GCSE Geography

EXAM REVISION NOTES

Jane Ferretti
Brian Greasley

Philip Allan Updates, part of the Hodder Education Group, an Hachette Livre UK company, Market Place, Deddington, Oxfordshire OX15 0SE

Orders
Bookpoint Ltd, 130 Milton Park, Abingdon, Oxfordshire, OX14 4SB
tel: 01235 827720
fax: 01235 400454
e-mail: uk.orders@bookpoint.co.uk
Lines are open 9.00 a.m.–5.00 p.m., Monday to Saturday, with a 24-hour message answering service. You can also order through the Philip Allan Updates website: www.philipallan.co.uk

© Philip Allan Updates 2001

ISBN 978-0-86003-441-4

Design by Juha Sorsa
Cover illustration by Neil Fozzard
Printed in Singapore

Philip Allan Updates' policy is to use papers that are natural, renewable and recyclable products and made from wood grown in sustainable forests. The logging and manufacturing processes are expected to conform to the environmental regulations of the country of origin.

About this book

Revision is vital for success in your GCSE examination. No-one can remember what they learnt up to 2 years ago without a reminder. To be effective, revision must be planned. This book provides a carefully planned course of revision — here is how to use it.

The book	*The route to success*
Contents list	**Step 1** Check which topics you need to revise for your examination. Mark them clearly on the contents list and make sure you revise them.
Revision notes	**Step 2** Each section of the book gives you the facts you need to know for a topic. Read the notes carefully, and list the main points.
Key words	**Step 3** Key words are given at the end of each information page and highlighted in the text. Learn them and their meanings. They must be used correctly in the examination.
Case study	**Step 4** Each section has a case study. Learn one for each topic. You could do this by listing the main headings with key facts beneath them on a set of revision cards. If your teacher has taught different case studies, use the one you find easiest to remember.
Test yourself	**Step 5** A set of brief questions is given at the end of each section. Answer these to test how much you know. If you get one wrong, revise it again. You can try the questions before you start the topic to check what you know.
Examination questions	**Step 6** Examples of questions are given for you to practise. Notice the higher-tier question at the end for those entered for the higher tier. The more questions you practise, the better you will become at answering them.
Exam tips	**Step 7** The exam tips offer advice for achieving success. Read them and act on the advice when you answer the question.
Key word index	**Step 8** On pp. 117–118 there is a list of all the key words and the pages on which they appear. Use this index to check whether you know all the key words. This will help you to decide what you need to look at again.

Command words

All examination questions include **command** or **action** words. These tell you what the examiner wants you to do. Here are some of the most common ones.

◆ **List** — usually wants you to provide a list of facts.

◆ **Describe** — requires more than a list. For example, you are expected to write a description of the pattern of population in Wales, but *not* to give any explanation for it.

◆ **Explain**, **give reasons for** or **account for** — here the examiner is expecting you to show understanding by giving reasons, and to do more than describe, for example, the pattern of population in Wales.

◆ **Suggest** — the examiner is looking for sensible explanations, using your geographical knowledge, for something to which you cannot know the actual answer — for example, 'Suggest reasons for the location of the factory in photograph A'.

◆ **Compare** — the best candidate will not write two separate accounts of the factors to be compared, but will pick several points and compare them one at a time. Useful phrases to use are 'whereas', 'on the other hand', 'compared to'.

Do you know?

The exam board setting your paper?

↓

What level or tier you will be sitting?

↓

How many papers you will be taking?

↓

The date, time and place of each paper?

↓

How long each paper will be?

↓

What the subject of each paper will be?

↓

What the paper will look like? Do you write your answer on the paper or in a separate booklet?

↓

How many questions you should answer?

↓

Whether there is a choice of questions?

↓

Whether any part of the paper is compulsory?

↓

If you don't know the answer to any of these questions as the exam approaches – ask your teacher!

Revision rules

Start early.

↓

Plan your time by making a timetable.

↓

Be realistic – don't try to do too much each night.

↓

Find somewhere quiet to work.

↓

Revise thoroughly – reading is not enough.

↓

Summarise your notes, make headings for each topic, and list the case study examples.

↓

Ask someone to test you.

↓

Try to answer some questions from old papers. Your teacher will help you.

↓

If there is anything you don't understand – ask your teacher.

Be prepared

The night before the exam

Complete your final revision.

↓

Check the time and place of your examination.

↓

Get ready your pens, pencil, coloured pencils, ruler and calculator (if you are allowed to use one).

↓

Go to bed early and set the alarm clock!

On the examination day

Don't rush.

↓

Double check the time and place of your exam and your equipment.

↓

Arrive early.

↓

Keep calm – breathe deeply.

↓

Be positive.

Examination tips

Keep calm and concentrate.

↓

Read the paper through before you start to write.

↓

If you have a choice, decide which questions you are going to answer.

↓

Make sure you can do all parts of the questions you choose, including the final sections.

↓

Complete all the questions.

↓

Don't spend too long on one question at the expense of the others.

↓

Stick to the point and answer questions fully.

↓

Use all your time.

↓

Check your answers.

↓

Do your best.

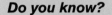

Plate tectonics

The Earth's crust is made up of pieces like a jigsaw, called **tectonic plates**.

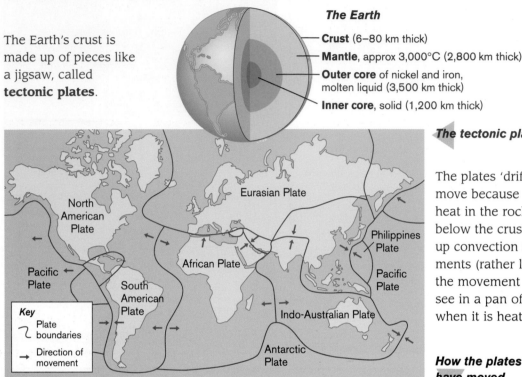

The Earth

Crust (6–80 km thick)

Mantle, approx 3,000°C (2,800 km thick)

Outer core of nickel and iron, molten liquid (3,500 km thick)

Inner core, solid (1,200 km thick)

The tectonic plates

Eurasian Plate

North American Plate

Philippines Plate

Pacific Plate

African Plate

Pacific Plate

South American Plate

Indo-Australian Plate

Antarctic Plate

Key

⌐ Plate boundaries

→ Direction of movement

The plates 'drift' or move because the heat in the rock below the crust sets up convection move-ments (rather like the movement you see in a pan of soup when it is heated).

How the plates have moved

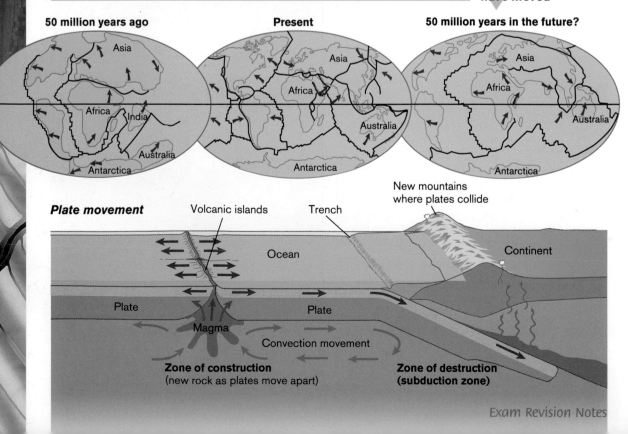

50 million years ago

Asia

Africa India

Australia

Antarctica

Present

Asia

Africa

Australia

Antarctica

50 million years in the future?

Asia

Africa

Australia

Antarctica

Plate movement

Volcanic islands

Trench

New mountains where plates collide

Ocean

Continent

Plate

Plate

Magma

Convection movement

Zone of construction
(new rock as plates move apart)

Zone of destruction
(subduction zone)

Types of plate margin

Plates meet at plate margins. There are four different types.

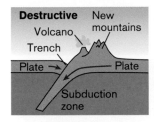

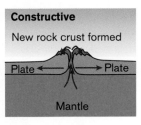

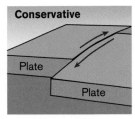

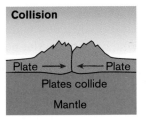

A **destructive plate margin** occurs where one plate slides beneath another as they collide. The bottom plate crumples, creating new mountains and volcanoes

At a **constructive plate margin** the plates are moving apart. Molten rocks from the mantle below spread out and harden, forming a ridge of new rock

At a **conservative plate margin** the plates slide past each other. Pressure builds up until they move with a 'jerk', causing earthquakes

A **collision plate margin** is where two plates collide and are crushed against each other. They are pushed upwards, forming new mountains

Fold mountains

When tectonic plates collide, huge forces cause the rocks to be folded and buckled, forming mountains like the Andes in South America and the Himalayas in Asia.

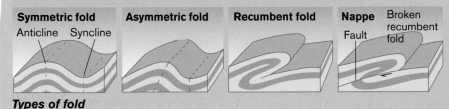

Types of fold

An upfold is called an **anticline**. A downfold is called a **syncline** (remember sink = down).

Rocks

There are three main types of rock:

Igneous rocks are formed when molten magma cools. If it cools beneath the surface, large crystals have time to grow and granite is formed. If it flows to the surface, quicker cooling results in basalt.

Sedimentary rocks are usually made of fine material deposited in lakes and seas. Sandstone is formed from sand compressed by the weight of other deposits on top of it. Chalk and limestone are formed from millions of shells of tiny sea creatures.

Metamorphic rocks occur when igneous or sedimentary rocks are changed by great heat or pressure from volcanic eruptions or mountain building. In this way chalk and limestone are changed to marble.

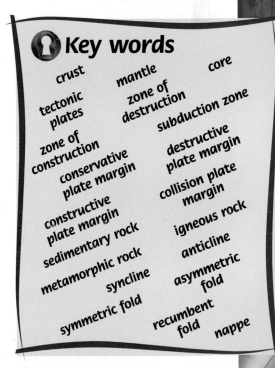

🔑 Key words

crust
mantle
core
tectonic plates
zone of destruction
subduction zone
zone of construction
conservative plate margin
destructive plate margin
constructive plate margin
collision plate margin
sedimentary rock
igneous rock
metamorphic rock
anticline
syncline
asymmetric fold
symmetric fold
recumbent fold
nappe

Earthquakes

Earthquakes and volcanoes are examples of natural hazards which occur on the plate margins.

Earthquakes are usually the result of plate movement, which is not smooth. The strain builds up along a fault line between two plates until they move, causing earthquakes.

The point where the earthquake starts below the Earth's surface is known as the **focus**. The point directly above the focus on the Earth's surface is known as the **epicentre**.

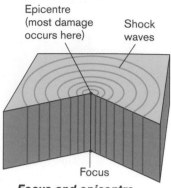

Focus and epicentre

Measuring earthquakes

The magnitude of an earthquake is recorded by an instrument called a **seismometer**. It measures the height of the shock waves on the **Richter scale**. Each point on the scale is 10 times greater than the one below. This means that an earthquake with a score of 7 is 10 times more powerful than one with a score of 6. The seismometer records the earthquake vibrations with a pen on a sensitive arm, marking zigzag lines on a drum of paper.

The **Mercalli scale**, which has been largely replaced by the Richter scale, measures the strength of an earthquake by its observed effects on buildings. So 1 on the Mercalli scale would only be detectable by seismographs and there would be no damage at all, while 12 would be catastrophic, with no buildings left standing.

Precautions against earthquakes

Individuals
- prepare an emergency pack including water, food, blankets, first aid kit, radio, torch
- during and after the earthquake, shelter under a table or bed, avoid stairways
- turn off gas, water and electricity
- after the earthquake move to open ground

Authorities
- monitor the hazard so people can be warned
- have emergency supplies ready
- make plans for shelter, food and water supplies, for emergency services, fire brigade, police, ambulance, and hospital services
- plan to broadcast information for people affected

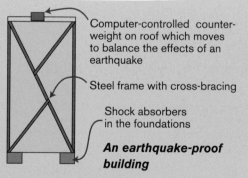

Computer-controlled counter-weight on roof which moves to balance the effects of an earthquake

Steel frame with cross-bracing

Shock absorbers in the foundations

An earthquake-proof building

Long-term planning
- ensure road and rail communications are built to reduce the effect of earthquakes
- ensure all new buildings are earthquake-proof

Can we predict earthquakes?

American experts using the latest equipment can measure very small plate movements and record the strain building up. They can predict that an earthquake will occur but not when it will happen.

Case study: Kobe, Japan

- ◆ The earthquake at Kobe struck on 17 January 1995.
- ◆ It measured 7.2 on the Richter scale.
- ◆ Japan lies at the margins of three plates, on a destructive plate margin and subduction zone.
- ◆ The epicentre was in Osaka Bay, close to the cities of Osaka and Kobe.

The location of Kobe

Primary effects

- ◆ Violent shaking of the earth and buildings for 20 seconds.
- ◆ Aftershocks lasting half an hour.
- ◆ Over 5,000 people killed and 25,000 injured.
- ◆ Gas mains fractured, electricity cut off, many fires started.
- ◆ Water mains broken so no water reaching houses.
- ◆ 200,000 buildings collapsed, leaving 300,000 homeless.
- ◆ Transport links disrupted, the elevated motorway in downtown Kobe collapsed, and railway lines blocked, making the job of the emergency services very difficult.

Secondary effects

- ◆ Transport disrupted for weeks afterwards.
- ◆ Older houses worst hit, new earthquake-proof buildings survived better. Heavy cost of rebuilding, which takes years to complete.
- ◆ Water and food shortages, so army brought supplies to people living in schools.

Effects of earthquakes in LEDCs

Lack of services so there are limited medical supplies and hospitals to deal with injured

If LEDCs require foreign aid to cope with the aftermath, it takes time to arrive

Communications are poor: access roads are poorly maintained and in remote areas people may not have radios

The people are not prepared and do not know what to do in the emergency

Why the effects of earthquakes in LEDCs are often worse than in MEDCs

Housing is built using traditional methods and is not earthquake-proof

Without adequate water the spread of disease is a constant danger

There are few plans for dealing with the emergency, which means delays in bringing emergency services to the area

There are few experts available to give advice and assess the situation

Key words

Richter scale

Mercalli scale

epicentre

focus

seismometer

Volcanoes

Molten rock known as **magma** can escape when pressure builds up below the Earth's surface. When the magma reaches the surface it is known as **lava**.

Volcanoes may erupt very explosively at destructive plate margins, releasing enormous amounts of lava, ash and steam. Sometimes lava is more liquid and flows more gently to the surface through cracks in the crust at constructive plate margins.

Types of volcano

Active volcanoes are those which have erupted recently and are likely to erupt again.

Dormant volcanoes are those which have not erupted for a long time but may erupt again.

Extinct volcanoes are unlikely ever to erupt again.

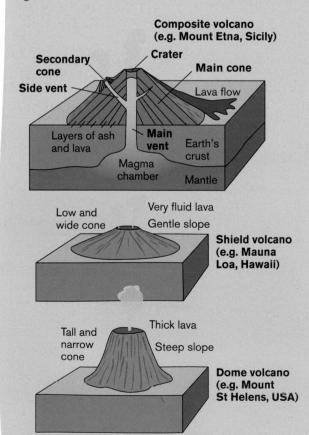

Composite volcano
(e.g. Mount Etna, Sicily)

Secondary cone
Crater
Main cone
Side vent
Lava flow
Layers of ash and lava
Main vent
Earth's crust
Magma chamber
Mantle

Low and wide cone
Very fluid lava
Gentle slope
Shield volcano (e.g. Mauna Loa, Hawaii)

Tall and narrow cone
Thick lava
Steep slope
Dome volcano (e.g. Mount St Helens, USA)

Volcano facts

◆ When a volcano erupts violently it throws ash and **volcanic bombs**, which are pieces of rock, into the air.

◆ Hot gases, ash and steam can form **pyroclastic flows** which move very fast and can cause tremendous damage.

◆ When a volcano has been dormant for some time the magma in the vent acts as a **plug**. When the volcano erupts the plug is blown out, often blowing off the top of the cone and leaving a very large crater known as a **caldera**.

◆ Mud flows called **lahars** are formed when hot ash melts snow and ice or falls into rivers. They move very fast and are very destructive.

◆ There are over 600 active volcanoes in the world.

🔑 Key words

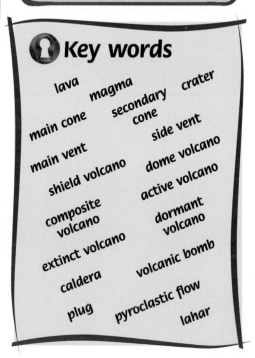

lava magma crater
main cone secondary cone
main vent side vent
shield volcano dome volcano
composite volcano active volcano
extinct volcano dormant volcano
caldera volcanic bomb
plug pyroclastic flow lahar

Case study:
Mount St Helens, USA

- ◆ Mount St Helens was a popular tourist area for fishing, climbing and walking.
- ◆ It lies at the margins of the North American Plate and the Pacific Plate. This is a destructive zone.
- ◆ The volcano erupted on 18 May 1980, having been dormant since 1857. Scientists had warned of the eruption and most people were evacuated.

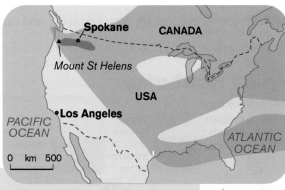

Map showing location of Mount St Helens and area covered by ash cloud

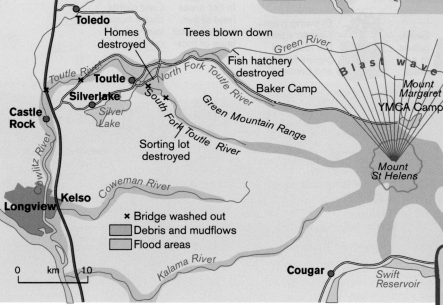

Map showing the effects of eruption in the local area

- ◆ The eruption was so violent that the top of the mountain was blown off with a blast greater than a 20 kilotonne atomic bomb. A great caldera was left.
- ◆ The blast covered 400 km², throwing trees over ridges 500 metres high.
- ◆ Hot ash and gas flowed down the slopes at 160 km/hour, melting snow and ice and forming destructive lahars.
- ◆ The ash cloud crossed the USA in 3 days and circled the globe in 17 days.
- ◆ The eruption left 100 people dead, including a geologist at an observation post 8 km away.

People often live near volcanoes because the ash produces fertile soil and good crops.

On Mount Etna in Sicily people have tried diverting the flows of lava away from villages by building dams. They have only been partially successful.

Water supply and demand in Britain

There is plenty of water to supply the population of Britain. However, there is more water in areas of low population density, such as Scotland and northwest England, than there is in the south and east where most people live.

The map shows that Welsh Water **abstracts** by far the most water, and that largely this is **surface water** (**reservoirs** and rivers). On the other hand, Southern, Anglian and Wessex abstract much less water and rely on ground-water supplies for up to 75%. These companies supply three of the most densely populated areas of the country. In hot and dry summers, some water companies find it difficult to supply all their customers. All of them are worried about how they will meet future demand.

The demand for water is steadily growing as more houses are built and industry expands. People are using more and more water at home in washing machines and dish-washers, for cleaning the car and watering the garden. Industries too use more water every year. Supplying enough water in the future could be a problem, especially if global warming brings longer, hotter and drier summers.

Attempts to solve the problem include:
- Building new reservoirs such as Carsington Water in Derbyshire and Kielder Water in Northumberland.
- Reducing the amount of water lost due to leaking pipes. This is over 25% in some areas.
- Constructing a National Water Grid (similar to the electricity grid) so water can be transferred from areas with **surplus** to areas with a shortage or **deficit**.
- Persuading people to use less water.

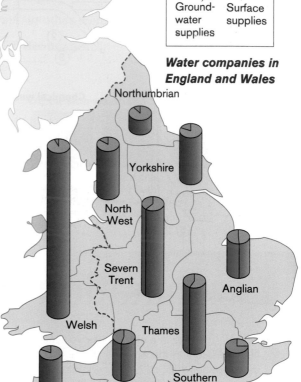

Key
Total abstraction (million litres/day)

2,000 —
1,000 —
0 —

Ground-water supplies | Surface supplies

Water companies in England and Wales

Northumbrian
Yorkshire
North West
Severn Trent
Anglian
Welsh
Thames
Southern
Wessex
South West

0   km   200

Key words

abstract
surface water
reservoir
surplus
deficit

Case study:
Carsington Water, Derbyshire

Carsington Water reservoir was built by Severn Trent Water authority in 1991 to improve the supply of water for its customers. It is an example of a water management scheme. The site at Carsington was chosen because:

◆ it is on impermeable rock
◆ there was enough water from local streams to fill the reservoir
◆ it didn't cause too much disruption to local people (only two farms were flooded)

A huge earth dam was built to hold back the water in the reservoir. All the clay and rock used for the dam wall was dug out of the valley which later became the reservoir. The stone used for facing the outside of the wall was obtained from local quarries. The project cost £107 million.

The reservoir holds 36,284 million litres of water. In the dry summers of 1995 and 1996 it helped Severn Trent to maintain supplies when other water companies, like Yorkshire Water, were unable to do so

The main purpose is to store water during wet weather and to guarantee water supply during dry weather

In winter, when there is plenty of water in the River Derwent, it is pumped out of the river at Ambergate along a 10 kilometre aqueduct (pipe) to the reservoir, where it is stored

In summer, when the river is lower, water flows out of the reservoir back to the river. This ensures that there is always enough water in the River Derwent

The water is abstracted (taken out of the river) at Little Eaton pumping station and piped to Derby and other towns

Matlock

Wirksworth

River Derwent

Water transfer

Carsington Water

Ambergate

Belper

N

Little Eaton

Derby

0   km   10

The Carsington water management scheme

Impacts on people

◆ The reservoir provides a reliable source of water for thousands of people.
◆ There is less chance of flooding in the River Derwent valley.
◆ There are activities for visitors (over 1 million people a year) including walks, cycle hire, water sports, fishing, a restaurant and a playground.
◆ Jobs have been created, initially in building the reservoir and now looking after visitors.

Impacts on the environment

◆ There is a completely new landscape — agricultural land has been replaced by the reservoir.
◆ The ecosystem has changed, but the water has attracted a wide variety of wildlife.
◆ A new road has been built for access. This means extra traffic and some pollution.
◆ Visitors can damage the environment, for example by dropping litter and causing footpath erosion.

The hydrological cycle

The hydrological cycle or the water cycle is the continuous movement of water between the land, the sea and the atmosphere.

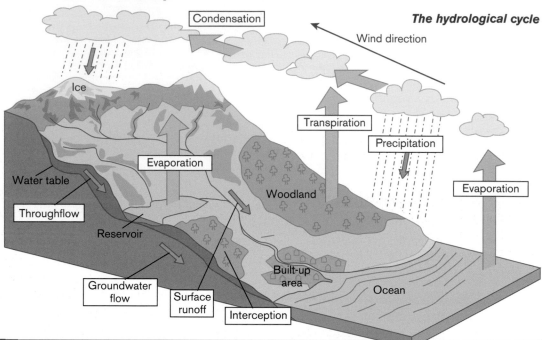

The hydrological cycle

Precipitation All water released from clouds such as rain, snow, hail, sleet and fog.

Surface runoff Water flowing across the surface. The water may be in a channel, such as a river or stream, or it may be **overland flow** when it makes its way across a field or down a roadway.

Interception When water collects on objects such as leaves or flat roofs.

Infiltration When water soaks into soil.

Throughflow When water soaks into soil and seeps through it towards a river or the sea.

Percolation The downward movement of water through soil into rocks.

Groundwater flow The movement of water below the water table. Water which is stored underground is called groundwater.

Evaporation When water which is heated by the sun becomes vapour and rises into the atmosphere. This may take place over land or sea.

Transpiration All plants lose water through their leaves. Transpiration is when this water returns to the atmosphere where it evaporates.

Evapotranspiration The term for the processes of both evaporation and transpiration.

Condensation When water vapour is cooled and turns into water droplets to form clouds.

Water table The upper level of saturated ground. It is not a 'table'. It is not even flat. The level is closer to the surface in winter when there is plenty of rain.

The drainage basin

The **drainage basin** is the area of land drained by a river and its **tributaries**. Large rivers such as the Nile or Mississippi have vast drainage basins. The boundary of a drainage basin is called the **watershed**. This is usually a range of hills or mountains. Rain falling beyond the watershed will flow into another river and is part of another drainage basin.

A drainage basin can also be represented in a systems diagram such as the one below. This shows how water is held in stores and how it is transferred between stores.

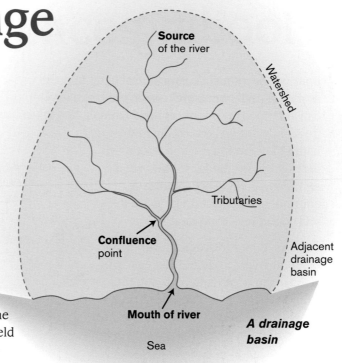

A drainage basin

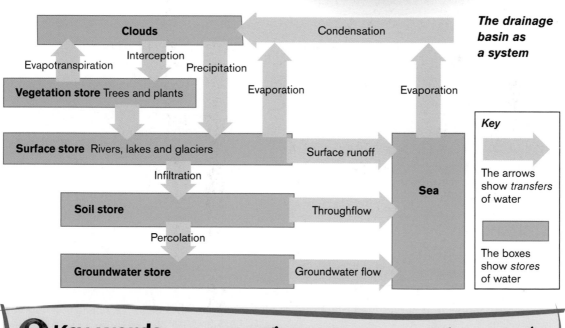

The drainage basin as a system

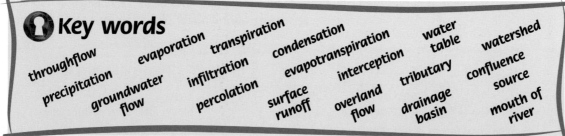

Key words

throughflow evaporation transpiration condensation evapotranspiration water table watershed

precipitation groundwater flow infiltration percolation surface runoff interception overland flow tributary drainage basin confluence source mouth of river

Flooding

If a river overflows its banks and inundates the surrounding land it is called a flood. Many rivers flood, some frequently, others less so, and often with little warning. Severe floods can destroy homes, bridges, power lines and food supply. They can cause enormous disruption to people's lives and sometimes even death.

The shape of a hydrograph varies for different rivers in different areas. The steeper the ascending limb, the more likely the river is to flood because it shows the amount of water in the river rising very quickly. If the ascending limb is gentle, flooding is less likely.

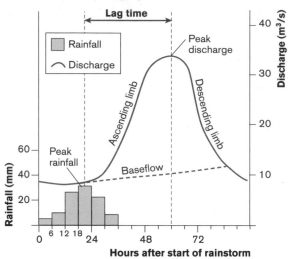

A storm hydrograph

The storm **hydrograph** shows river discharge, which is the amount of water in a river. You can see how **discharge** changes over a short period after a rainstorm.

Wooded areas

This hydrograph has a gentle ascending limb because:

◆ Trees and leaves intercept rain so it is less likely to reach the river.
◆ The ground surface is soft and water easily infiltrates it, so reducing surface runoff.
◆ The water table is low because trees take up the soil moisture.

Flooding is unlikely in wooded areas.

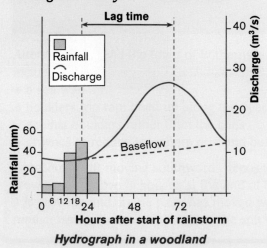

Hydrograph in a woodland

Urban areas

This hydrograph has a steep ascending limb because:

◆ Much of the ground surface is covered by tarmac or concrete and is impermeable. This means there is little infiltration and a lot of surface runoff.
◆ Drains carry rainwater to the river very quickly.

Flooding is more likely in an urban area.

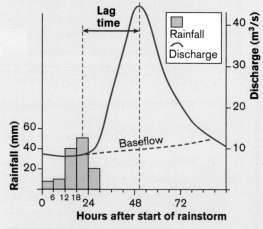

Hydrograph in an urban area

Flood control

17

rivers and water

It is difficult to prevent floods, especially when they happen with little warning. However, new technology means that river levels are carefully monitored, so flooding can be predicted and warnings given to people living in areas likely to be flooded. In Britain, this is the job of the Environment Agency. The risk of flooding can also be reduced by:

◆ Planting trees (**afforestation**) in the upper catchment. However, this changes the appearance and ecosystem of the area.
◆ Building a dam and reservoir. This is a very effective way of controlling flooding, and the new lake can be used for recreation and even for generating hydroelectricity. However, this is expensive. It leads to loss of land and sometimes displaces a lot of people as in the Three Gorges Dam project in China (see p. 108).

Natural flood control

Natural flood control entails:
◆ Setting embankments back from the channel to allow flooding around the river.
◆ Planting water-loving plants, such as willow and alder. This helps to lower the water table and increases the amount of wildlife.
◆ Digging a flood relief channel so the river can cope with increased discharge when necessary. In normal conditions, the meandering river course is maintained.

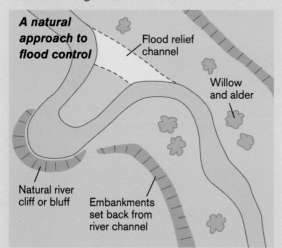

A natural approach to flood control. Flood relief channel. Willow and alder. Natural river cliff or bluff. Embankments set back from river channel.

The natural approach enhances the environment and can provide access for people to enjoy the river and its surroundings. Natural solutions to flood control are less expensive to implement and maintain than hard engineering solutions.

Hard engineering

Hard engineering entails:
◆ Building embankments, also called 'dykes' or 'levées'. These raised banks increase the capacity of the channel and keep flood waters in the river.
◆ Straightening and deepening the river. Water flows more quickly along a straight channel, reducing the risk of flooding. However, areas further downstream may be at greater risk because the floodwaters reach them more quickly. The river will revert to its natural course unless the new channel is reinforced continually.

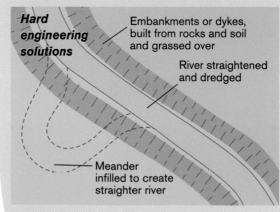

Hard engineering solutions. Embankments or dykes, built from rocks and soil and grassed over. River straightened and dredged. Meander infilled to create straighter river.

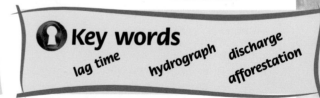

🔒 Key words

lag time   hydrograph   discharge   afforestation

River processes

Like glaciers and the sea, rivers are important agents of **erosion**, **transport** and **deposition**.

Erosion

Rivers erode in four main ways:

Hydraulic action The power of running water undercuts the banks and erodes the bed.

Abrasion or corrasion Rocks and pebbles carried by the river crash against the sides and bed of the river, scraping away material.

Attrition Rocks and pebbles carried by the river bang into each other and break up into smaller pieces.

Solution or corrosion Some minerals from rocks are dissolved and carried away by the river, e.g. calcium carbonate.

Waterfall retreats upstream as supporting shale is eroded, and a gorge develops downstream

Whinstone hard rock

Waterfall develops where there is a band of (whinstone) hard rock

Shale

Plunge pool

Erosion of softer shale below hard rock causes undercutting

River Tees

High Force on the River Tees

As the waterfall erodes, it moves slowly upstream, leaving a steep gorge on the lower side of the falls.

The upper course of the river

Rivers usually rise in hills or mountains. The river flows quickly towards the sea, carrying large amounts of **sediment** downstream. The river's course is not straight. It flows around interlocking spurs of higher land. There is a lot of bedload and many large rocks are angular in shape. Waterfalls are a common feature in this part of the river.

Transport

Rivers transport an enormous load. This material can be carried in four ways:

Traction Boulders and rocks are dragged or rolled along the river bed.

Saltation Smaller-sized particles, such as pebbles or sand, are bounced along the bed.

Suspension Fine particles of silt or clay are held in the water.

Solution Minerals are dissolved in the river water.

Cross-section through a river

Suspended load

Dissolved load Material dissolved in the water which cannot be seen

Bed load Pebbles, rocks and boulders are rolled or bounced along the channel bed

Stones become smaller and rounded as they are moved due to attrition

The middle and lower course of the river

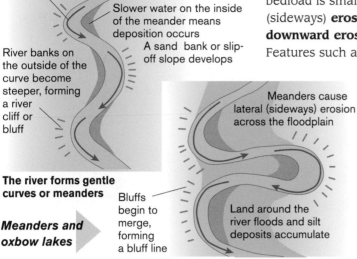

The fastest water (current) on the outside of the bend causes erosion

Slower water on the inside of the meander means deposition occurs

A sand bank or slip-off slope develops

River banks on the outside of the curve become steeper, forming a river cliff or bluff

The river forms gentle curves or meanders

Meanders and oxbow lakes

Bluffs begin to merge, forming a bluff line

Meanders cause lateral (sideways) erosion across the floodplain

Land around the river floods and silt deposits accumulate

Meanders grow much larger

As the river flows through lower-lying land it flows faster and with less turbulence. The bedload is smaller and rounder. **Lateral** (sideways) **erosion** is more important than **downward erosion**, but deposition also occurs. Features such as meanders, oxbow lakes, flood-plains and levées develop.

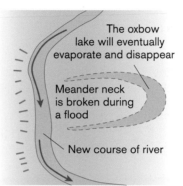

The oxbow lake will eventually evaporate and disappear

Meander neck is broken during a flood

New course of river

Meander is cut off from the main channel, usually during a flood. An oxbow lake is formed

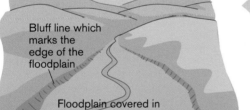

River floodplain

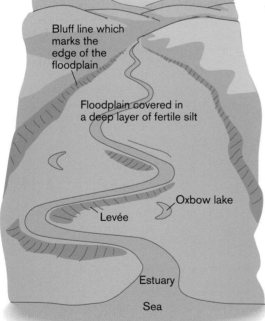

Bluff line which marks the edge of the floodplain

Floodplain covered in a deep layer of fertile silt

Oxbow lake

Levée

Estuary

Sea

Deposition

A river drops its load when it no longer has enough energy to carry it. The larger, heavier material is deposited first, and this is seen higher up the river. Pebbles, gravel, sand and silt are deposited in the middle and lower course. The dissolved load is not deposited but is carried out to sea.

The mouth of the river

As the river enters the sea, it tends to form a wide funnel shape, called an **estuary**. This part of the river is tidal and has a mixture of fresh-water and salt water. Deposition of fine silt and clay around the estuary can form extensive mudflats and salt marshes.

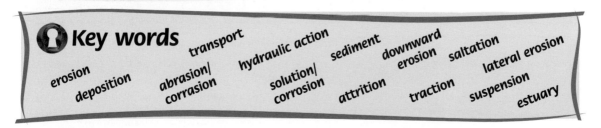

🔑 **Key words**

transport

erosion

deposition

abrasion/ corrasion

hydraulic action

solution/ corrosion

sediment

attrition

downward erosion

traction

saltation

lateral erosion

suspension

estuary

Deltas

Some rivers have a **delta**. This forms when silt accumulates at the mouth of the river, especially during flooding, and the sea is unable to remove it. There are three types of delta:

- **arcuate or fan-shaped**, e.g. the Niger (Nigeria)
- **cuspate**, e.g. the Ebro (Spain)
- **bird's foot**, e.g. the Mississippi (USA)

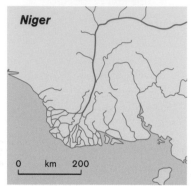
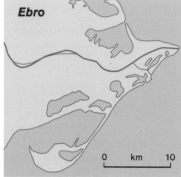

 Case study: How the Nile Delta has changed

Since the completion of the Aswan High Dam in 1970 huge quantities of silt have been trapped behind the dam in Lake Nasser. Consequently, not enough silt reaches the delta. This has the following serious consequences:

- The delta is getting smaller and people have lost their homes and land.
- Valuable nutrients are lost and fish stocks have gone down.
- The soil is less fertile without the annual replenishment of silt. Farmers must now buy artificial fertilisers for their land. These are expensive and can cause pollution.

The delta stretches approximately 160 km in each direction

The Mediterranean Sea is shallow and has no tide. It does not have enough energy to remove the silt

Alexandria

Port Said

Suez Canal

The river forms **distributaries** as it flows through the delta

0   km   100

Cairo

Red Sea

The River Nile carries a huge amount of silt as it approaches the sea. The silt contains a lot of nutrients, so makes good farm land. Fish thrive in the nutrient-rich water. The silt which has accumulated over centuries has formed a flat and fertile delta which is now a densely settled area

 Key words   delta   distributary   cuspate delta   arcuate/fan-shaped delta   bird's foot delta

Test yourself

1 Which is the odd one out in each of these groups of words? Explain why in each case.

   precipitation, infiltration, clouds

   groundwater flow, throughflow, surface runoff

   baseflow, lag time, peak discharge

   embankment, reservoir, canal

   meander, delta, floodplain

2 Draw a diagram to show how a waterfall is formed.

3 True or false? Explain your answer in each case.

   Flooding is more likely in built-up areas.

   Britain is short of water.

   The point where a tributary joins the main river is called a confluence.

   The level of the water table rarely changes.

   Saltation is another term for the suspended load in a river.

   The River Nile and the River Mississippi both have large deltas.

 Exam tip

If you are asked to write about a landform, you must choose a feature made on the land, e.g. a delta or a flood-plain. Meanders and oxbow lakes are water features.

Examination question

(a) **Name features A, B and C on the diagram.** (3 marks)

(b) **Explain the formation of an oxbow lake using diagrams to help you.** (4 marks)

Foundation tier:

(c) (i) **Name a river you have studied where flooding has been a problem.**
(ii) **Explain what caused the floods to occur.**
(iii) **Describe what steps have been taken to protect people and buildings from the flooding.** (8 marks)

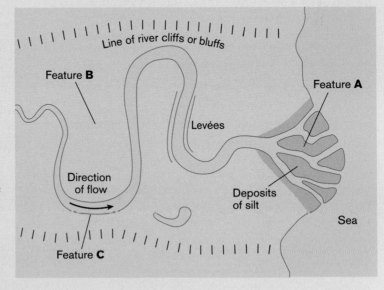

Higher tier:

(d) **Using one or more examples you have studied, explain how river flooding can be prevented.** (8 marks)

Ice sheets

In some areas of the world the snow which falls never entirely melts. Areas such as Antarctica in the south, Greenland and Arctic Canada in the north, and highland regions such as the Alps and Himalayas, are permanently covered in snow and ice. Such large frozen areas are known as **ice sheets**.

During the ice ages such ice sheets covered the whole of northern Britain.

Areas of Britain covered by ice during the ice ages

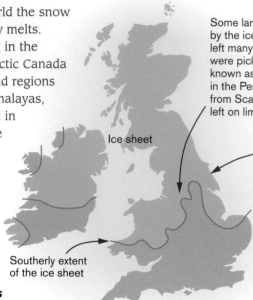

Ice sheet

Southerly extent of the ice sheet

Some large pieces of rock were carried by the ice and, when it melted, were left many kilometres from where they were picked up. These rocks are known as **erratics**. At Brimham Rocks in the Pennines large boulders brought from Scandinavia by the ice have been left on limestone rocks

Boulder clay which had been carried by the ice was left over large areas of eastern Britain. It was scraped along underneath the ice sheet as clay, and often contained boulders of various sizes. Boulder clay is a type of **till**. Where this soft clay forms cliffs, for example on the Holderness coast, it is rapidly eroded (see p. 32)

Erosion by ice

As snow builds up, its surface may thaw and freeze repeatedly. When the snowflakes thaw and refreeze they form a whitish grain-like snow called **firn**. The weight of more snow falling on top forces out more air, and the firn granules merge to form bluish **glacier ice**. This ice eventually moves down the mountainside and forms a **glacier**.

Ice is a powerful agent of erosion in three ways:

Freeze–thaw Water in small cracks in rock will freeze. As it freezes it expands and widens the cracks. Repeated freezing and thawing will cause rocks to shatter.

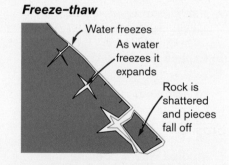

Freeze–thaw

Water freezes

As water freezes it expands

Rock is shattered and pieces fall off

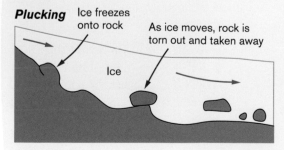

Plucking Ice freezes onto rock

As ice moves, rock is torn out and taken away

Ice

Plucking Ice freezes onto rock and when the ice moves it pulls a piece of rock away.

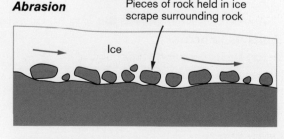

Abrasion

Pieces of rock held in ice scrape surrounding rock

Ice

Abrasion Pieces of rock carried by the ice scrape at the surrounding rock and erode it away.

A glacier

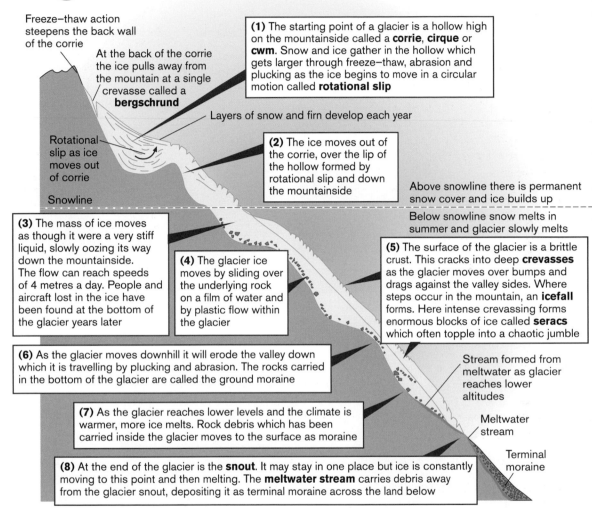

Freeze–thaw action steepens the back wall of the corrie

At the back of the corrie the ice pulls away from the mountain at a single crevasse called a **bergschrund**

Rotational slip as ice moves out of corrie

Snowline

Layers of snow and firn develop each year

(1) The starting point of a glacier is a hollow high on the mountainside called a **corrie**, **cirque** or **cwm**. Snow and ice gather in the hollow which gets larger through freeze–thaw, abrasion and plucking as the ice begins to move in a circular motion called **rotational slip**

(2) The ice moves out of the corrie, over the lip of the hollow formed by rotational slip and down the mountainside

Above snowline there is permanent snow cover and ice builds up

Below snowline snow melts in summer and glacier slowly melts

(3) The mass of ice moves as though it were a very stiff liquid, slowly oozing its way down the mountainside. The flow can reach speeds of 4 metres a day. People and aircraft lost in the ice have been found at the bottom of the glacier years later

(4) The glacier ice moves by sliding over the underlying rock on a film of water and by plastic flow within the glacier

(5) The surface of the glacier is a brittle crust. This cracks into deep **crevasses** as the glacier moves over bumps and drags against the valley sides. Where steps occur in the mountain, an **icefall** forms. Here intense crevassing forms enormous blocks of ice called **seracs** which often topple into a chaotic jumble

(6) As the glacier moves downhill it will erode the valley down which it is travelling by plucking and abrasion. The rocks carried in the bottom of the glacier are called the ground moraine

Stream formed from meltwater as glacier reaches lower altitudes

Meltwater stream

Terminal moraine

(7) As the glacier reaches lower levels and the climate is warmer, more ice melts. Rock debris which has been carried inside the glacier moves to the surface as moraine

(8) At the end of the glacier is the **snout**. It may stay in one place but ice is constantly moving to this point and then melting. The **meltwater stream** carries debris away from the glacier snout, depositing it as terminal moraine across the land below

Erosion
As the glacier moves downhill it will erode the valley by abrasion and plucking, smoothing away ridges and deepening the valley.

Transportation
The glacier will carry a large amount of rock debris known as **moraine**. This varies in size from rocks as large as a house to powder called **rock flour**. Most of the load is near the glacier base.

Deposition
At the snout the ice melts and its load is dumped in piles or washed away by the meltwater to be deposited over the lowland.

🔑 Key words

ice sheet plucking erratic firn

glacier ice abrasion till

corrie/cirque/cwm rotational slip freeze–thaw

rock flour meltwater stream bergschrund

icefall snout glacier crevasse serac

Glaciated landscapes

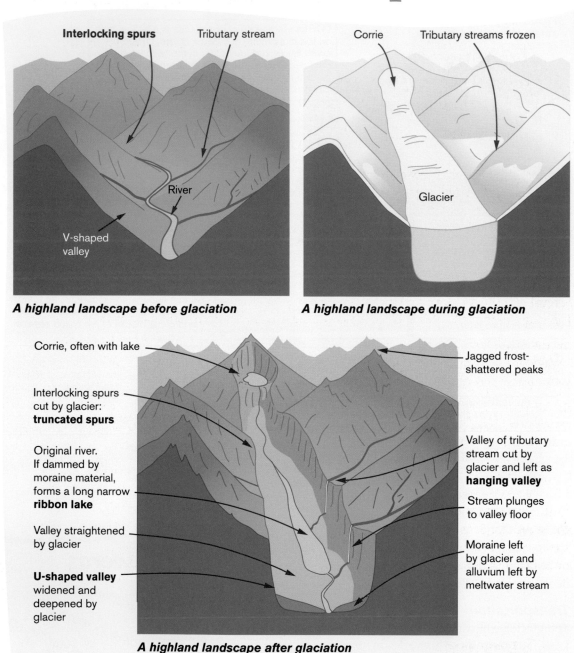

A highland landscape before glaciation

Interlocking spurs

Tributary stream

River

V-shaped valley

A highland landscape during glaciation

Corrie

Tributary streams frozen

Glacier

A highland landscape after glaciation

Corrie, often with lake

Jagged frost-shattered peaks

Interlocking spurs cut by glacier: **truncated spurs**

Valley of tributary stream cut by glacier and left as **hanging valley**

Original river. If dammed by moraine material, forms a long narrow **ribbon lake**

Stream plunges to valley floor

Valley straightened by glacier

U-shaped valley widened and deepened by glacier

Moraine left by glacier and alluvium left by meltwater stream

Fjords are long narrow inlets where a U-shaped valley has reached the coast and become filled with sea water as the glacier melted. They can be up to 160 kilometres long, only 8 kilometres wide, and extremely deep. They often have a shallow entrance where the terminal moraine is located.

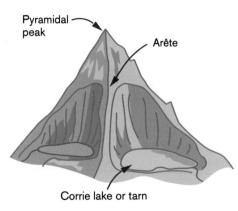

Pyramidal peak

Arête

Corrie lake or tarn

Pyramidal peak A sharp peak formed when three or more corries are created back to back.

Arête A steep knife-edged ridge which separates two corries.

Tarn A lake formed in the bottom of the corrie.

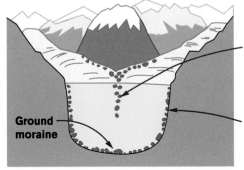

Cross-section of a glacier

Medial moraine: rocks carried in the middle of the glacier where two glaciers meet

Ground moraine

Lateral moraine: rocks carried at the sides of the glacier

Moraine is the material eroded from the sides and floor of the valley and carried by the glacier down the mountains.

Lowland areas

Lateral, **medial** and **terminal moraines** are left as long, low hills in the landscape. The material in meltwater streams, usually sand and gravel, forms **outwash plains**.

Drumlins are long, low hills deposited in lowland areas, shaped when seen from above like the back of a spoon.

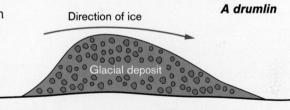

A drumlin

Direction of ice

Glacial deposit

Roches moutonées are formed where there is an outcrop of hard rock. As the glacier moves over the rock it smoothes (by abrasion) the side facing the flow and plucks the rock from the other side. The abrasion leaves scratches or **striations** on the rock. Roche moutonée is French for 'sheep rock', because the feature looks like a sheep sitting down.

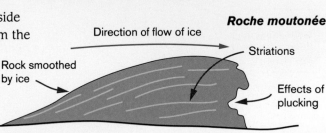

Roche moutonée

Direction of flow of ice

Striations

Rock smoothed by ice

Effects of plucking

🔒 Key words

ground moraine
medial moraine
lateral moraine
truncated spurs
interlocking spurs
terminal moraine
arête
ribbon lake
pyramidal peak
hanging valley
roche moutonée
drumlin
striations
U-shaped valley
fjord
outwash plain

Case study:
Snowdonia, north Wales

Snowdon (1,085 metres) is the highest mountain in England and Wales and the centrepiece of the Snowdonia National Park. It is a good example of a glaciated landscape. On the map below, the heavy green lines show the main ridges (many are arêtes) enclosing the semi-circular hollows (cwms).

Physical features

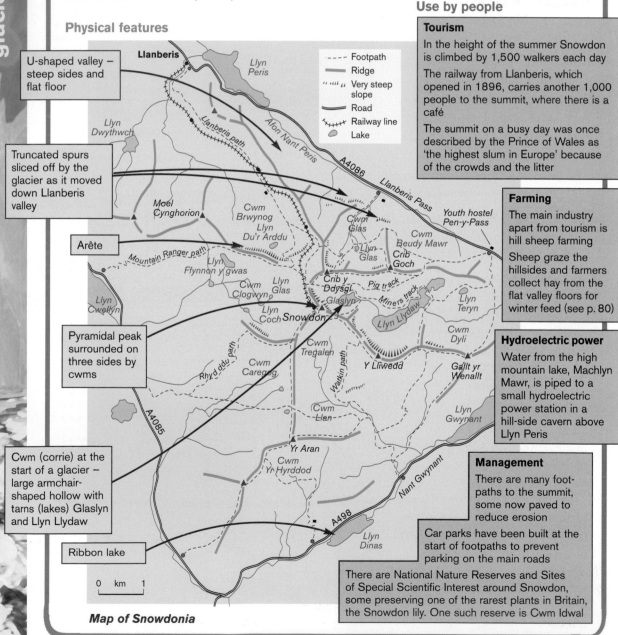

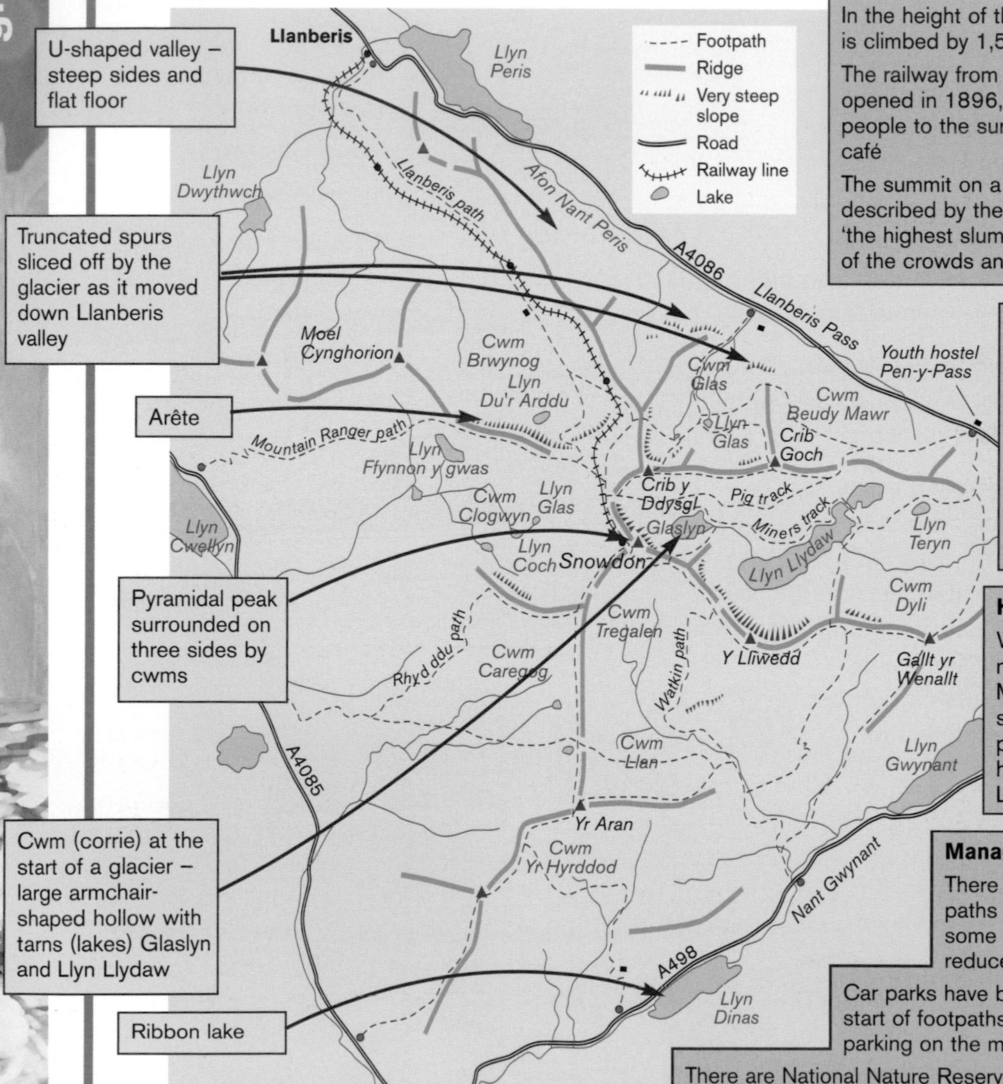
U-shaped valley – steep sides and flat floor
Truncated spurs sliced off by the glacier as it moved down Llanberis valley
Arête
Pyramidal peak surrounded on three sides by cwms
Cwm (corrie) at the start of a glacier – large armchair-shaped hollow with tarns (lakes) Glaslyn and Llyn Llydaw
Ribbon lake
Footpath
Ridge
Very steep slope
Road
Railway line
Lake
Llanberis
Llyn Peris
Llyn Dwythwch
Llanberis path
Afon Nant Peris
A4086
Llanberis Pass
Youth hostel Pen-y-Pass
Moel Cynghorion
Cwm Brwynog
Llyn Du'r Arddu
Cwm Glas
Llyn Glas
Cwm Beudy Mawr
Crib Goch
Mountain Ranger path
Llyn Ffynnon y gwas
Cwm Clogwyn
Llyn Glas
Crib y Ddysgl
Pig track
Miners track
Glaslyn
Llyn Teryn
Llyn Cwellyn
Llyn Coch
Snowdon
Llyn Llydaw
Cwm Dyli
Rhyd ddu path
Cwm Caregog
Cwm Tregalen
Watkin path
Y Lliwedd
Gallt yr Wenallt
A4085
Cwm Llan
Llyn Gwynant
Yr Aran
Cwm Yr Hyrddod
Nant Gwynant
A498
Llyn Dinas
0 km 1

Map of Snowdonia

Use by people

Tourism

In the height of the summer Snowdon is climbed by 1,500 walkers each day

The railway from Llanberis, which opened in 1896, carries another 1,000 people to the summit, where there is a café

The summit on a busy day was once described by the Prince of Wales as 'the highest slum in Europe' because of the crowds and the litter

Farming

The main industry apart from tourism is hill sheep farming

Sheep graze the hillsides and farmers collect hay from the flat valley floors for winter feed (see p. 80)

Hydroelectric power

Water from the high mountain lake, Machlyn Mawr, is piped to a small hydroelectric power station in a hill-side cavern above Llyn Peris

Management

There are many foot-paths to the summit, some now paved to reduce erosion

Car parks have been built at the start of footpaths to prevent parking on the main roads

There are National Nature Reserves and Sites of Special Scientific Interest around Snowdon, some preserving one of the rarest plants in Britain, the Snowdon lily. One such reserve is Cwm Idwal

Test yourself

Match the correct word from the list on the right to each description.

1 Pieces of rock frozen in the ice scraping at the surrounding rock and wearing it away.

2 Ice freezing onto the rock and pulling it away when the glacier moves.

3 Large areas of ice and snow.

4 A hollow on the mountainside left by ice.

5 A single crevasse at the back of a corrie.

6 Enormous blocks of ice caused by intense crevassing.

7 A moraine formed at the side of a glacier.

8 A moraine formed in the centre of a glacier when two glaciers meet.

9 The lowest point of a glacier.

10 A knife-edged ridge between two corries.

11 A valley left high above the main valley floor.

12 A long, low hill of deposited material found in lowland areas.

hanging valley

lateral moraine

plucking

snout

ice field

bergschrund

abrasion

medial moraine

drumlin

seracs

corrie

arête

Examination question

(a) Look at the diagram below.

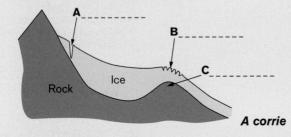

Rock **Ice**

A corrie

(i) Name the features A, B and C on the diagram.   (3 marks)
(ii) Label clearly the position of an arête in the diagram.   (1 mark)
(iii) Label clearly the direction in which the ice is moving.   (1 mark)
(iv) Explain fully how a corrie is formed.
                                                                  (5 marks)

Foundation tier:

(b) Look at the information opposite about tourism and management on Snowdon.
   (i) Give two reasons why some people would be in favour of limiting the number of people visiting the mountain each day.   (4 marks)
   (ii) What other steps (apart from limiting numbers) can the authorities take to limit the effects of tourism?
                                                                  (5 marks)

Higher tier:

(b) Explain why some people feel that beautiful areas like Snowdonia are in danger from tourism, and how the effects of too many tourists can be managed.   (9 marks)

 Exam tip

Remember to use the correct geographical terms in your explanation, for example in part (a) (iv) words like 'abrasion', 'freeze–thaw' and 'plucking'. In the higher-tier question don't forget to use your case-study knowledge to give examples of the points you make.

Waves and erosion

Two basic factors affect the nature of the coastline: the waves and the type of rock.

Waves

The movement of water particles in a wave is circular.

Direction of movement

When the wave reaches the shore the circle is broken and the wave spills forward — it breaks.

If the slope of the shore is shallow, the wave spills forward for a long distance and is called a **constructive wave** because it pushes material onto the beach.

If the slope of the shore is steep, the wave plunges down and hits the shore with great force. It is called a **destructive wave** because it erodes the coast.

Constructive wave

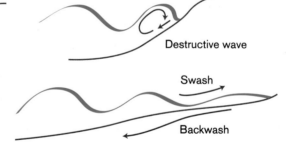

Destructive wave

As the wave breaks, it swills up the beach. This is known as **swash**. It then runs straight back down the beach — known as **backwash**.

Swash

Backwash

Type of rock

Hard rock, such as chalk and limestone, is difficult for the weather and sea to erode, so it stands out as hills and headlands.

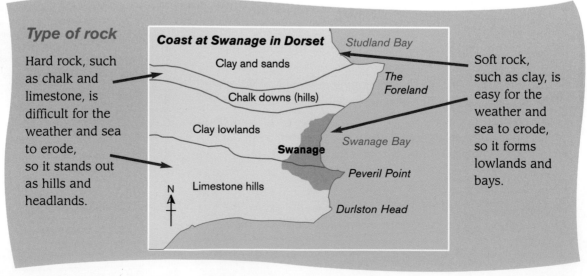

Coast at Swanage in Dorset — *Studland Bay*

Clay and sands

The Foreland

Chalk downs (hills)

Clay lowlands

Swanage Bay

Swanage

Peveril Point

N

Limestone hills

Durlston Head

Soft rock, such as clay, is easy for the weather and sea to erode, so it forms lowlands and bays.

Processes of erosion by waves

Waves erode the coastline in four main ways.

Abrasion or corrasion The sea hurls pebbles and sand against the base of the cliff, chipping and grinding it down.

Hydraulic action Powerful waves lash the cliffs, forcing air into tiny cracks. The pressure of the compressed air weakens the rock and forces it to break up.

Corrosion The sea water may react with chemicals and minerals in some rocks and they can be dissolved.

Attrition The rocks and stones which the sea erodes from the cliffs are rounded and broken down as they bump against each other and they are thrown against the cliff.

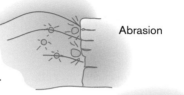

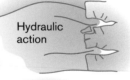

Erosion of cliffs

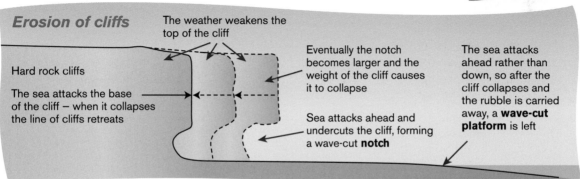

The weather weakens the top of the cliff

Hard rock cliffs

The sea attacks the base of the cliff – when it collapses the line of cliffs retreats

Eventually the notch becomes larger and the weight of the cliff causes it to collapse

Sea attacks ahead and undercuts the cliff, forming a wave-cut **notch**

The sea attacks ahead rather than down, so after the cliff collapses and the rubble is carried away, a **wave-cut platform** is left

Erosion of a headland

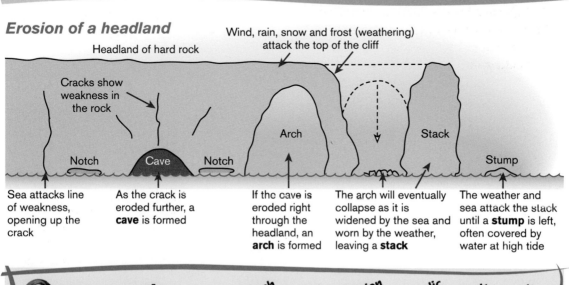

Headland of hard rock

Wind, rain, snow and frost (weathering) attack the top of the cliff

Cracks show weakness in the rock

Notch | Cave | Notch | Arch | Stack | Stump

Sea attacks line of weakness, opening up the crack

As the crack is eroded further, a **cave** is formed

If the cave is eroded right through the headland, an **arch** is formed

The arch will eventually collapse as it is widened by the sea and worn by the weather, leaving a **stack**

The weather and sea attack the stack until a **stump** is left, often covered by water at high tide

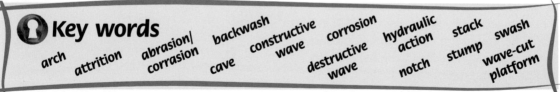

🔑 Key words

arch · attrition · abrasion/corrasion · backwash · cave · constructive wave · corrosion · destructive wave · hydraulic action · notch · stack · stump · swash · wave-cut platform

Waves and deposition

The material eroded from cliffs by the sea is worn down by the process of attrition and is moved by the sea to be deposited further along the coast. The sea moves material by **longshore drift**.

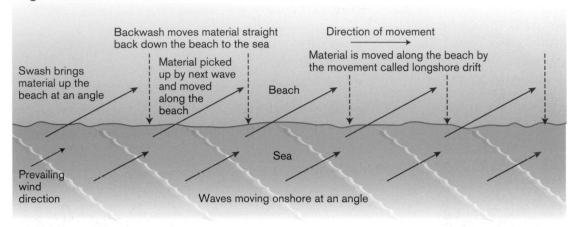

Backwash moves material straight back down the beach to the sea

Direction of movement

Swash brings material up the beach at an angle

Material picked up by next wave and moved along the beach

Material is moved along the beach by the movement called longshore drift

Beach

Prevailing wind direction

Sea

Waves moving onshore at an angle

Features created by longshore drift

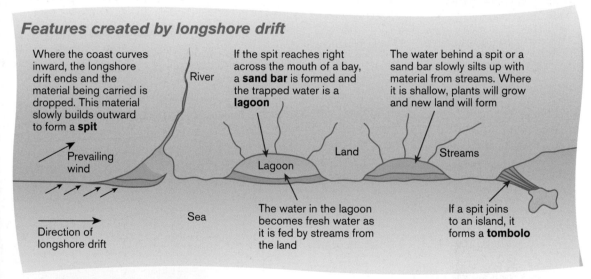

Where the coast curves inward, the longshore drift ends and the material being carried is dropped. This material slowly builds outward to form a **spit**

River

If the spit reaches right across the mouth of a bay, a **sand bar** is formed and the trapped water is a **lagoon**

The water behind a spit or a sand bar slowly silts up with material from streams. Where it is shallow, plants will grow and new land will form

Prevailing wind

Land

Streams

Lagoon

Direction of longshore drift

Sea

The water in the lagoon becomes fresh water as it is fed by streams from the land

If a spit joins to an island, it forms a **tombolo**

Coastal defences: groynes

At seaside resorts wooden walls or groynes are built across the beach to stop the sand being washed away by longshore drift. The beach material builds up at one side of the groyne. Trapping the material like this may cause problems elsewhere as it stops the material moving down the coast where, for instance, it may be building up and protecting the base of a cliff.

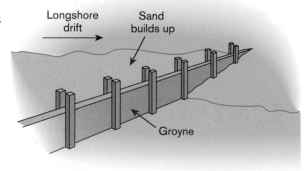

Longshore drift

Sand builds up

Groyne

Coastal defences

Where the sea is eroding the coastline it can do so at an alarming rate. This may not be seen as an issue when farmland is involved, but if homes and towns are threatened then it is more serious. The most common methods used to try and stop the erosion are:

Sea walls The most effective method of halting sea erosion. They are also the most expensive. Made of concrete, they are curved to deflect the power of the waves. But the sea can undermine them if the beach material in front of them is not maintained.

Concrete sea wall curves outwards to deflect the force of the waves

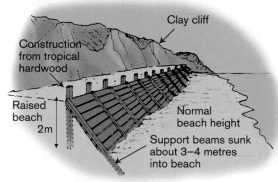

Clay cliff

Construction from tropical hardwood

Raised beach 2m

Normal beach height

Support beams sunk about 3–4 metres into beach

Revetments Sloping wooden fences with an open structure of planks to break the force of the waves and trap beach material behind them, protecting the base of the cliffs. They are cheaper but not as effective as sea walls.

Gabions Less expensive than a sea wall or a revetment. They are cages of boulders built up at the foot of the cliff or on a sea wall.

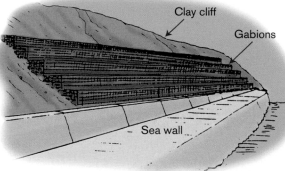

Clay cliff

Gabions

Sea wall

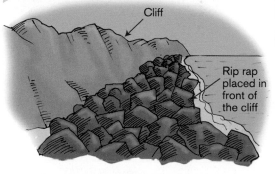

Cliff

Rip rap placed in front of the cliff

Rip rap The cheapest method. It entails placing piles of large boulders on the beach to protect the cliffs from the full force of the sea.

Sea defences such as these are very expensive to build and maintain and are only used when towns, villages or expensive installations are at risk.

🔑 **Key words**

lagoon

longshore drift

revetment

rip rap

sand bar

spit

gabion

groyne

sea wall

tombolo

Case study: The east coast and Spurn Head

The coast between Flamborough Head and Spurn Head is formed of boulder clay, a soft rock which is easily eroded by the sea. Four kilometres of land has been eroded in the last 2,000 years. There are two main reasons for this rapid erosion:

◆ Boulder clay is soft rock and is eroded by both the weather and the sea.
◆ Longshore drift sweeps the eroded material south so that no beach builds up in front of the cliffs to protect them.

Attempts have been made to keep the beach at Mappleton by building a wall or large groyne out from the shore. This has helped to retain sand. It means that places further south on the coast have less sand to protect their cliffs and so erosion has increased rapidly.

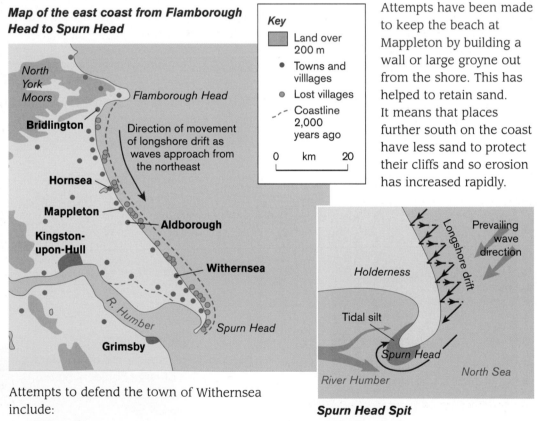

Map of the east coast from Flamborough Head to Spurn Head

Key
- Land over 200 m
- Towns and villlages
- Lost villages
- Coastline 2,000 years ago

0   km   20

Spurn Head Spit

Attempts to defend the town of Withernsea include:

◆ a sea wall
◆ boulders (rip rap) lined up along the beach to reduce the wave energy — waves break against boulders rather than the cliffs
◆ groynes to reduce longshore drift and build up sand on the beach

Longshore drift moving southwards deposits material at Spurn Head. The Humber lifeboat crew and pilot live in houses at the end of the spit. It is not stable. There is evidence that it is growing and, in the past, has moved westwards as the coastline has retreated. The road crossing the narrow 'neck' of the spit was washed away in 1991.

Test yourself

1 Tick those statements which are correct and put a cross next to those which are incorrect.

(a) A constructive wave spills forward on a gently-sloping coast, pushing material onto the beach. ☐

(b) Soft rock such as clay is easy for the weather and sea to erode, so it forms headlands. ☐

(c) Corrosion is the process by which the sea hurls pebbles at the cliffs, wearing them down. ☐

(d) Attrition is the process by which rocks from the cliffs are rounded and broken down. ☐

(e) A wave-cut platform is left at the base of a cliff after the cliff has collapsed. ☐

(f) When a headland arch collapses a notch is left standing offshore. ☐

(g) The zigzag movement of the swash and backwash causes longshore drift. ☐

(h) If material builds across the mouth of a bay due to longshore drift it forms a sand spit. ☐

(i) Groynes are built to prevent longshore drift washing away the sand at a seaside resort. ☐

(j) Gabions are a more expensive method of preventing cliff erosion than revetments. ☐

2 Label the diagrams below correctly and give each a title.

Title: ....

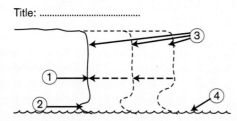

Title: ....

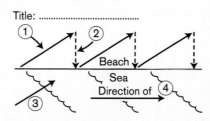

> ## ▲ Exam tips
>
> ◆ Make sure you have learnt and can use a case study for the final part of the question.
> ◆ The higher-tier question has four parts in the sentence – can you find them?

Examination question

(a) (i) Label the diagram:

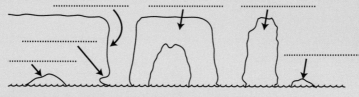

(3 marks)

(ii) Describe two ways in which the sea wears away the coast. (2 marks)

(iii) Explain how the top of the cliff is worn away. (2 marks)

(iv) Explain why headlands are formed. (2 marks)

Foundation tier:

(b) (i) Give a named example of a place where people have tried to stop the sea wearing away the coast. (1 mark)

(ii) Describe how the people in your named example tried to stop the sea wearing away the coast. (4 marks)

(iii) Explain why they used this method and not any other. (4 marks)

Higher tier:

(b) Using a named example, explain how people have tried to stop the sea eroding the coast and outline the advantages and disadvantages of the method chosen. (8 marks)

Weather and climate

It is important to know the difference between the two words **weather** and **climate**.

Weather means day-to-day changes in atmospheric conditions. Words like sunny, warm, cloudy, rainy, windy or snowy are ways of describing the weather. We can talk about the weather today, yesterday or last week — 'weather' is used to describe fairly short-term events. It is something you might write about on a holiday postcard: 'the weather is lovely and sunny'.

Weather forecasts predict the weather over the next few days. This one from a daily newspaper shows a rather wet and windy day in prospect, with temperatures ranging from 1°C in Scotland to 6°C in southern England.

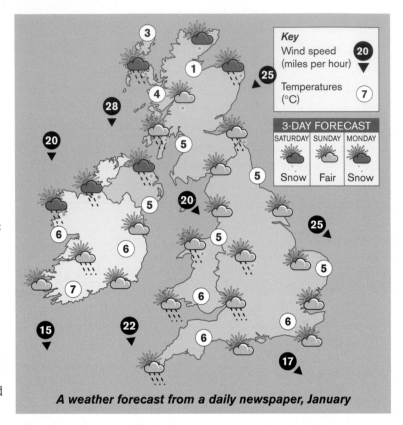

A weather forecast from a daily newspaper, January

Climate is the pattern of weather over a year. It is put together by taking the average conditions for a period of 40 years.

When describing the climate of an area you can include:
◆ the pattern of precipitation during the year (this might be snow or sleet as well as rain)
◆ the total precipitation for the year
◆ the average monthly temperature
◆ the range in temperature
◆ average sunshine hours per month
◆ average wind speeds and direction

Climate is often shown using a climate graph such as this one for Nottingham, England.

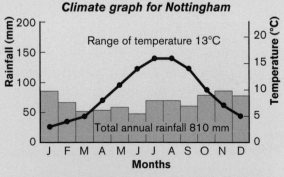

Climate graph for Nottingham

Winters are mild with an average 3°C in January.

Rain in Britain falls throughout the year with a slight winter maximum.

Total rainfall in Nottingham averages 810 mm a year.

Summer temperatures are warm, reaching an average of 16°C.

Air masses

One reason why Britain has such change-able weather is that several different air masses affect the country. An air mass is a large body of air which has a similar temperature and humidity throughout. Air masses which come from the Atlantic Ocean carry a lot of moisture and often bring rain. Air from the continent of Europe is usually dry and brings more settled weather. Air flows from the south are generally warmer than those from the north.

The main air masses affecting Britain

Arctic air mass is less common than the others but can bring icy arctic air in winter, leading to very cold weather

Polar maritime air mass brings cold air and often rain or even snow in winter

Polar continental air mass blows across Scandinavia and the North Sea and brings cold dry weather. It may cause snow showers on the east coast because the air picks up moisture as it crosses the North Sea

Tropical maritime air mass brings warm and wet weather. This air mass is brought by southwest winds which are very common in Britain

Tropical continental air mass brings warm, dry weather

Rainfall in Britain

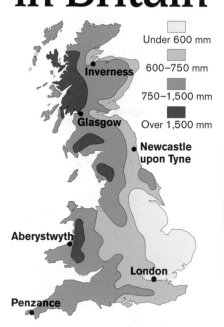

Under 600 mm

600–750 mm

750–1,500 mm

Over 1,500 mm

Inverness

Glasgow

Newcastle upon Tyne

Aberystwyth

London

Penzance

Britain is much wetter in the north and west than in the south and east, and high land has much more rain than low-lying land. Rainfall in the Scottish Highlands is over 1,500 mm a year whereas in London it is only about 600 mm a year.

Why it rains

Relief rainfall
Relief (orographic) rain helps to explain why north and west Britain are much wetter than the south and east. The **prevailing wind** in Britain is from the southwest and this brings moist air which cools as it is forced to rise over the Pennines, Welsh mountains and Scottish Highlands. Condensation causes clouds and rain.

Frontal rainfall
Frontal rain develops along weather fronts which form where two air masses meet. Warm moist air meeting cooler air at a warm front is forced upwards. As it rises it cools and the moisture condenses to form rain. Britain lies in an area where air masses frequently meet and so we get a lot of this type of rain.

Convectional rainfall
On sunny days air warms and rises. As it rises it cools and the water vapour in the air condenses to form clouds and rain. Convectional rainfall occurs less than the other two types of rain in Britain because it is caused by heat, but long hot summer days can lead to afternoon thunder storms, especially in southeast England.

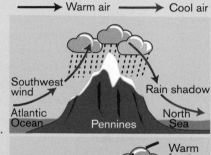

Warm air → Cool air

Southwest wind

Rain shadow

Atlantic Ocean

Pennines

North Sea

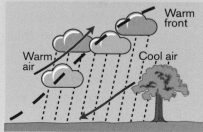

Warm front

Warm air

Cool air

Key words weather climate prevailing wind

Depressions

Depressions are low-pressure systems which bring changeable, usually rainy weather. They often develop to the west of Britain, where tropical and polar air masses meet, and travel eastwards across the country, blown by the prevailing westerly winds.

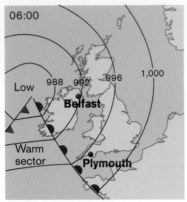

The depression is approaching Ireland

A depression crossing Britain

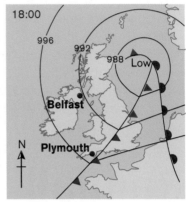

The depression has moved northeast and is now centred over western Scotland

The depression is moving away from Britain. The cold front is now lying across southeast England

A depression is recognisable on a weather map because of the two fronts, a warm front and a cold front, which meet at an apex. The **cold front** moves more quickly than the **warm front**, so the **warm sector** gradually becomes smaller. As the fronts merge an **occluded front** forms, often bringing particularly bad weather conditions.

As a depression crosses over the country it brings changeable weather.

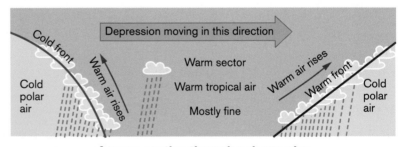

A cross-section through a depression

Hazards caused by depressions

Floods Heavy rain brought by a depression may lead to flooding. This is most likely when the depression is moving slowly, or if a lot of rain has fallen in preceding weeks.

Gales and strong winds Strong winds can cause serious damage to trees and buildings, and even deaths. In 1987 a devastating gale brought by a depression swept across southeast Britain.

Heavy snow and blizzards If depressions develop after a period of very cold weather they can cause heavy snow. This can block roads and bring down power lines, usually in northern England and Scotland.

Coastal flooding Depressions can cause very high tides called **storm surges.** These, together with large waves, can result in flooding of low-lying coastal areas such as the Thames Estuary. The Thames Barrier was built in 1982 to protect London from this type of flooding.

Anticyclones

Anticyclones are high-pressure systems. These large areas of descending air bring settled weather that can last for several days or weeks. Pressure in these systems is usually over 1,000 millibars. If they persist they are called 'blocking highs' because they block out depressions.

In winter anticyclones bring cold, clear, settled weather. Temperatures can remain well below freezing, though the days may be clear and sunny with few clouds. At night it gets even colder because the lack of cloud cover means heat is lost quickly. This weather can cause problems, especially icy roads. **Fog** may develop in early mornings.

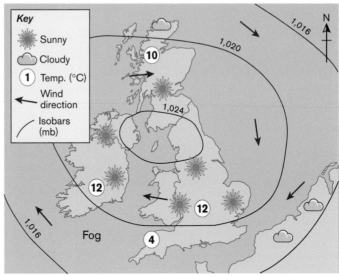

Key
- Sunny
- Cloudy
- (1) Temp. (°C)
- ← Wind direction
- Isobars (mb)

There are no weather fronts and this means that high pressure systems generally bring dry weather

The **isobars** are circular and spaced far apart, so the winds tend to be light and blow out from the centre in a clockwise direction

An anticyclone

In summer anticyclones bring hot, sunny days with temperatures up to 25°C or higher. At night temperatures fall rapidly because there is no cloud cover and this can cause a heavy morning dew. Another feature is thunderstorms occurring in the late afternoon of a hot day. These are caused by convection (see p. 35) and may be quite violent.

Hazards of summer anticyclones

Heatwaves Very high temperatures can be uncomfortable and even dangerous. People can become dehydrated or suffer heat stroke.

Drought Prolonged dry weather means demand for water may exceed supply. This happened in parts of the UK in summer 1997 when water shortages resulted in restrictions such as hose-pipe bans.

Forest or moorland fires If vegetation becomes very dry then serious fires can occur, as happened in the USA in summer 2000. Fires may be started by lightning or a carelessly discarded match. Damage can be extensive, destroying vegetation and animal habitats.

Pollution Sunshine can cause a build-up of pollutants in the atmosphere, especially in towns. When sunlight reacts with emissions from cars, ozone is created. This low-level ozone is a pollutant and can cause chest problems, especially asthma. The lack of wind in anticyclonic conditions means pollutants do not disperse.

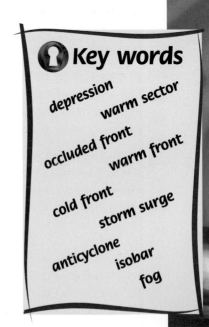

🔑 **Key words**

depression

warm sector

occluded front

warm front

cold front

storm surge

anticyclone

isobar

fog

Hurricanes

Hurricanes are intense low-pressure systems also known as typhoons and cyclones.

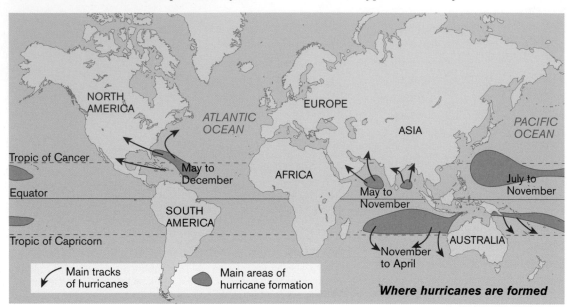

Where hurricanes are formed

Hurricanes develop in the tropics above a warm sea (over 27°C). They develop at the hottest time of year, between May and November in the northern hemisphere and between November and April in the southern hemisphere. Typical tracks of hurricanes are shown on the map.

Warm, damp air spirals upwards towards the top of the hurricane, which can be 20 kilometres high. As the air rises it cools and water vapour condenses, forming thick clouds. The central area has very low pressure, but it is calm and clear and is known as the eye of the storm. Very strong winds blow outwards from the eye, reaching up to 300 km per hour. Hurricanes also bring torrential rain and very high tides (a storm surge), both of which can cause severe flooding and landslides.

Hurricanes can be as much as 800 km in diameter, but the worst wind and rain is usually in a belt about 300 km wide. Weather satellites are used to track hurricanes, to try to warn people living in their paths, but warnings rarely give more than a few hours' notice. In LEDCs where communications are poor there may be very little warning at all.

Hurricanes need a warm sea to generate their energy, but once they reach land they quickly weaken and blow themselves out. This explains why places which are most affected by hurricanes are either islands or coastal areas.

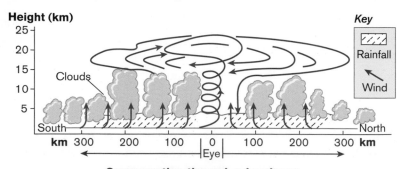

Cross-section through a hurricane

Case study: Hurricane Mitch

In November 1998 Hurricane Mitch devastated Honduras and Nicaragua, two of the world's poorest countries. It caused thousands of deaths and made hundreds of thousands of people homeless. Its long-term impacts will last well into the twenty-first century.

Mitch, which is one of the most violent hurricanes on record, developed in late October 1998 and was tracked across the Caribbean Sea. The people of Nicaragua and Honduras did not have much warning, and in any case could have done little to protect themselves.

Damage was caused by strong winds of up to 300 km per hour, high tides, large waves and heavy rain. The rain, which was unexpected and lasted 5 days, had the most severe impact. In some places over 1,000 mm fell, more rain in a week than they normally have in a year.

Most damage was caused by floods which swept away everything in their path and caused landslides. The floods destroyed towns, villages, roads, bridges and buildings including schools and hospitals. Some children in the region may now grow up without any education. In the weeks following the disaster there were serious food shortages and problems with disease as dead bodies were left to rot in the open,

Key The route of the centre of Hurricane Mitch, 22 October to 5 November 1998

Area affected by hurricane

Area affected by Hurricane Mitch

Nicaragua: 8,000 killed, over 700,000 homeless

Honduras: 17,000 killed, over 800,000 homeless

Mexico: 6 killed

Guatemala: 490 killed, 78,000 evacuated

El Salvador: 370 killed, 50,000 homeless

and water supplies became contaminated. Honduras has a total population of about 5 million and 800,000 people were made homeless.

Hurricane Mitch also devastated farmland. Coffee and banana plantations — two important export crops — were destroyed. It takes months for new plants to grow and this meant long-term problems for the economy. Even where crops could be harvested, the destruction of transport routes meant they could not be taken to the ports for export.

LEDCs such as Honduras and Nicaragua are too poor to build hurricane-proof structures like those you might find in Florida. Many of the houses destroyed in Honduras were flimsy buildings on steep slopes which were easily washed away. Early warning systems are also more difficult to manage in LEDCs and even if warnings are received there may be no means of escape.

Global warming

Global temperatures are rising. 1998 was the warmest year of the twentieth century and all but one of the warmest years on record have occurred since 1983. The world's leading scientists agree that this increase in global temperatures has largely been caused by the activities of people, especially in industrialised countries.

1 Sunlight passes through the atmosphere and warms the Earth

2 Heat is reflected back from Earth. Greenhouse gases in the atmosphere trap some heat and keep the Earth warm. Without this 'greenhouse effect', Earth would be too cold to support life

Atmosphere containing greenhouse gases

Global warming

3 People's activities are adding greenhouse gases to the atmosphere, so trapping more heat

Greenhouse gases
Carbon dioxide
Methane
CFCs
Nitrous oxide

People's activities are adding **greenhouse gases** such as carbon dioxide and methane to the atmosphere.

Burning fossil fuels in factories and power stations

Vehicle **emissions**

Release of chlorofluorocarbons (**CFCs**) from aerosols (now banned) and old refrigerators

Sources of greenhouse gases

Deforestation: forests are important because trees use up **carbon dioxide** in the process of photosynthesis. Removal of forests increases the amount of carbon dioxide in the atmosphere

> ### 📝 Exam tip
>
> *Make sure you under-stand the difference between the terms* **global warming** *and the* **greenhouse effect**.

The consequences

Increasing global temperatures are beginning to have effects all over the world.

◆ Weather patterns are changing. Britain will have wetter winters and warmer summers, and the USA will become drier.
◆ Sea levels will rise, causing flooding in low-lying areas such as Bangladesh and the Netherlands.
◆ There will be more violent storms and hurricanes, especially in tropical areas.
◆ Some wildlife may become extinct due to changed climatic conditions.

What is being done?

Nothing can be done to stop global warming, but action can be taken to slow it down in the future. This relies on a joint approach by all the large countries in the world, which is difficult to achieve. The Kyoto Agreement, signed by many countries in 1997, was an important step towards reducing emissions of greenhouse gases and most European countries are now taking action. The USA signed the Kyoto Agreement but is now reluctant to make any cuts, despite the fact that it produces at least 25% of the main polluting gases, because it is worried that cuts will damage its economy.

Case study: How will global warming affect Britain?

Key

20.5° Present July average temperature (°C)

(22.1°) July average temperature by 2050 (°C)

Areas liable to flooding as climate warms

John O'Groats 15.1° (16.7°)

Edinburgh 18° (19.6°)

Manchester 19° (20.6°)

London 20.5° (22.1°)

Paris

Climate zones are expected to move north steadily, giving London and the southeast the present climate of Paris by 2030–2050

0   km   100

The impact of global warming on Britain

◆ Rising sea levels of 20 to 40 cm mean low-lying areas will be flooded, for example the Fens and parts of the Thames Estuary.

◆ There will be more gales and storms, particularly in the winter. The winter of 2000/01 was the wettest since records began.

◆ Summers will be warmer and drier. Average temperatures may rise by 1.6°C by 2050. Farmers in the south will need to irrigate their crops. Water companies will have to store more water to meet increased demand.

◆ Britain could become a more popular holiday destination, pavement cafés could flourish and air conditioning will be needed in the south.

◆ There will be more rain and more likelihood of flooding in the autumn and winter. More money will have to be spent on flood protection, such as building embankments.

◆ Coniferous trees will grow more quickly, so up to 15% more wood will be produced, but deciduous trees could die from drought and disease.

◆ Vines, sunflowers and maize could be grown in the south.

◆ Insect pests could flourish.

The British government has agreed to cut emissions of greenhouse gases, particularly carbon dioxide, by:

◆ Using less coal and oil to generate electricity and using natural gas or renewable energy instead.

◆ Improving insulation in public buildings such as schools and hospitals.

◆ Persuading people to save energy by insulating their houses, turning lights out and only boiling as much water in the kettle as they need.

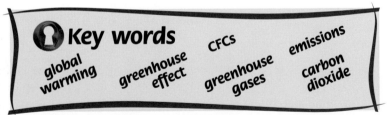

🔑 Key words

global warming   greenhouse effect   CFCs   greenhouse gases   emissions   carbon dioxide

Test yourself

1 What is the difference between 'weather' and 'climate'?
2 Draw diagrams to show how the three types of rainfall are formed (relief, convectional and frontal).
3 Name the main air masses affecting Britain and describe the typical weather associated with each.
4 What is meant by the term 'prevailing wind'?
5 How does the weather change as a depression (low-pressure system) passes over an area?
6 What sort of weather is associated with anticyclones (a) in the summer and (b) in the winter?
7 What do you understand by the term 'global warming'? How is Britain likely to be affected by global climate change?
8 What are hurricanes and where do they develop? In what ways do hurricanes cause damage to areas they cross?
9 Explain why the effects of hurricanes are often worse in LEDCs than in MEDCs.

Examination question

(a) **Shade the area of highest pressure.**
(1 mark)

(b) **Name the pressure system and use the information on the weather map to describe the weather being experienced in France (August).** (4 marks)

(c) **If this pressure system remained over France for several weeks, what kind of problems might develop?** (5 marks)

Foundation tier:
(d) (i) **Name three ways in which people are adding greenhouse gases to the atmosphere and increasing global warming.**
(ii) **Describe the effects global warming is likely to have on the environment.** (8 marks)

Higher tier:
(d) **Explain why climate change, such as global warming, may be more damaging to places in LEDCs than MEDCs.** (8 marks)

Weather map of France in August

Key
Wind speed (knots) and direction
Isobars (pressure in millibars)
27 Temp (°C)
0 km 200

Soils

Soil types vary all over the world. The type of soil depends largely on the climate, bedrock and vegetation in an area. For example, deciduous woodlands such as those found in Britain usually have deep fertile **brown earths**, tropical rainforests have reddish, clay soils called latosols, and coniferous forests typically have a grey-coloured **podzol**.

Soil is made up of weathered bedrock which contains minerals mixed with water, air and **humus** (decayed organic matter). Soil organisms such as bacteria, fungi and earthworms are important in keeping the soil fertile. Soil is also an important source of nutrients — the chemical elements such as nitrogen, calcium, magnesium and potassium which are essential for plant growth.

Nutrients may be lost from soils:
◆ In surface runoff — nutrients dissolve in water on the soil surface and are washed away.
◆ Through **leaching** — nutrients are washed into the lower layers of the soil, out of reach of plants. They may be re-deposited in the lower layers of the soil.

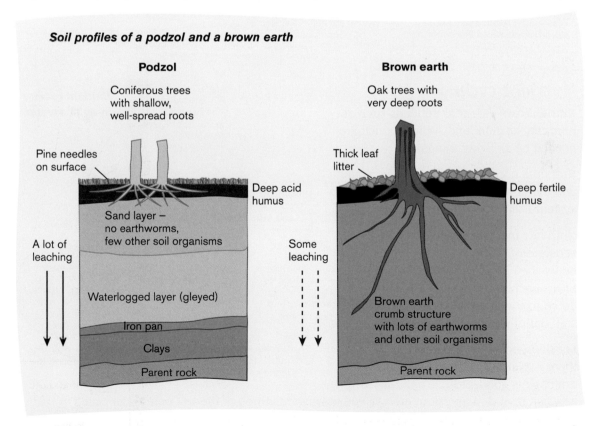

Soil profiles of a podzol and a brown earth

Podzol

Coniferous trees with shallow, well-spread roots

Pine needles on surface

Deep acid humus

Sand layer – no earthworms, few other soil organisms

A lot of leaching

Waterlogged layer (gleyed)

Iron pan

Clays

Parent rock

Brown earth

Oak trees with very deep roots

Thick leaf litter

Deep fertile humus

Some leaching

Brown earth crumb structure with lots of earthworms and other soil organisms

Parent rock

Key words   podzol   brown earth   leaching   humus

GCSE Geography

Ecosystems

An **ecosystem** consists of the plants and animals which live together in a particular environment. They depend on each other and on non-living parts of the environment such as rock and soils, water, sunlight and temperature.

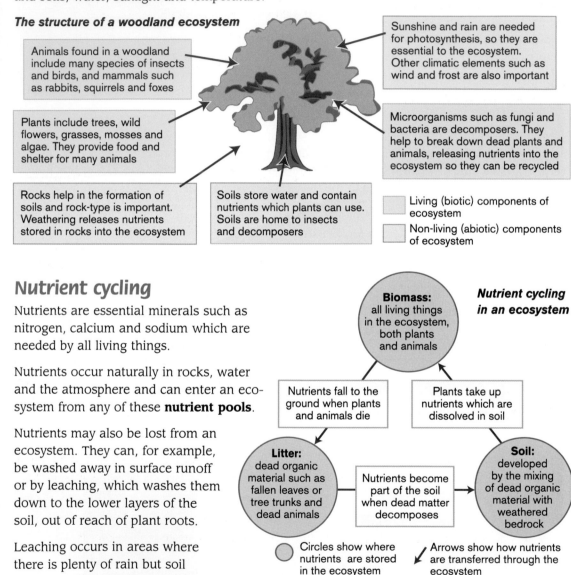

The structure of a woodland ecosystem

Animals found in a woodland include many species of insects and birds, and mammals such as rabbits, squirrels and foxes

Plants include trees, wild flowers, grasses, mosses and algae. They provide food and shelter for many animals

Rocks help in the formation of soils and rock-type is important. Weathering releases nutrients stored in rocks into the ecosystem

Soils store water and contain nutrients which plants can use. Soils are home to insects and decomposers

Sunshine and rain are needed for photosynthesis, so they are essential to the ecosystem. Other climatic elements such as wind and frost are also important

Microorganisms such as fungi and bacteria are decomposers. They help to break down dead plants and animals, releasing nutrients into the ecosystem so they can be recycled

Living (biotic) components of ecosystem

Non-living (abiotic) components of ecosystem

Nutrient cycling

Nutrients are essential minerals such as nitrogen, calcium and sodium which are needed by all living things.

Nutrients occur naturally in rocks, water and the atmosphere and can enter an ecosystem from any of these **nutrient pools**.

Nutrients may also be lost from an ecosystem. They can, for example, be washed away in surface runoff or by leaching, which washes them down to the lower layers of the soil, out of reach of plant roots.

Leaching occurs in areas where there is plenty of rain but soil drainage is good. Soluble salts such as calcium and magnesium are washed downwards through the soil and re-deposited in the lower layers. The upper layers become increasingly acid and less fertile.

Nutrient cycling in an ecosystem

Biomass: all living things in the ecosystem, both plants and animals

Nutrients fall to the ground when plants and animals die

Plants take up nutrients which are dissolved in soil

Litter: dead organic material such as fallen leaves or tree trunks and dead animals

Nutrients become part of the soil when dead matter decomposes

Soil: developed by the mixing of dead organic material with weathered bedrock

Circles show where nutrients are stored in the ecosystem

Arrows show how nutrients are transferred through the ecosystem

Gleying gives soils a distinctive blue colouring. It occurs where soils are not well drained, for example on gentle slopes and in hollows on impermeable rock. The waterlogged conditions cause iron salts to be chemically changed from a reddish to a grey-blue colour. Gleying is common in British soils, especially in boggy moorland areas like the Pennines.

Energy flow

All energy comes from the sun. Green plants use sunlight to make their own food (glucose) through the process of **photosynthesis**. Water and carbon dioxide are also essential for photosynthesis to occur. Green plants are known as primary producers because of their ability to produce food.

How do ecosystems function?

All ecosystems have two processes:
◆ the flow of energy through the system
◆ the cycling of nutrients

If either of these processes is disrupted, the whole ecosystem will be affected.

Energy is passed on from plants to all the animals in the ecosystem through **food chains** and **food webs**. This food energy is needed for all living processes such as growth, movement, respiration and reproduction.

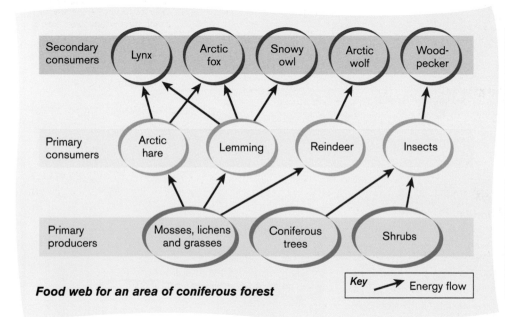

Food web for an area of coniferous forest

Key → Energy flow

What would happen to the number of arctic foxes if the lemming population decreased?

How would the food web be affected if acid rain damaged the trees and other plants?

The arrows show how energy is moved through the food web. Because every plant and animal uses up energy to live, there is less and less energy to be passed on. This is why a food chain rarely has more than five links.

Decomposers also obtain their energy from the food web, when plants and animals die. These organisms help in the process of decay which is important in the cycling of nutrients.

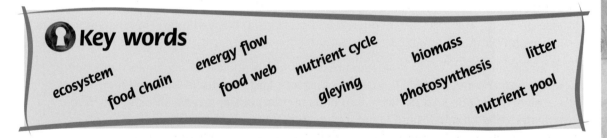

🔑 Key words

ecosystem   food chain   energy flow   food web   nutrient cycle   gleying   biomass   photosynthesis   litter   nutrient pool

Case study: Tropical rainforests

The map shows that the tropical rainforests extend around the world in a belt close to the equator. They flourish where the climate is hot and wet, typically with over 2,000 mm rain a year.

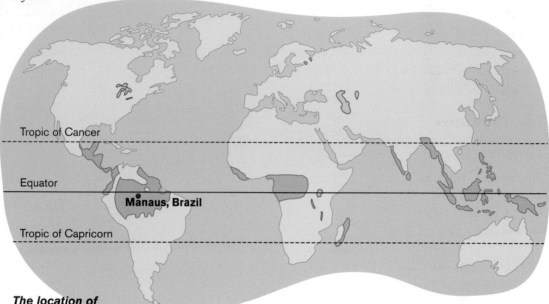

Tropic of Cancer

Equator

Manaus, Brazil

Tropic of Capricorn

The location of tropical rainforests

Temperatures are hot throughout the year – about 26 or 27°C.

Rainfall is heavy and mainly convectional in origin. Total rainfall is 1,773 mm.

It rains most days, usually in the afternoon.

No months are dry but there is a drier period between June and September.

There are no seasons. It is always hot and always wet.

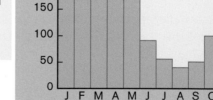

The climate graph for Manaus, Brazil

Range of temperature 1°C

Plants and animals

There are more plant and animal species in the rainforest than anywhere else on Earth. The forest is very dense and plant growth is vigorous. There are four layers of vegetation in the forest.

Tropical rainforests support vast numbers of animals, including mammals, birds and insects. Herbivores include thousands of insects, birds, squirrels, bats and monkeys. Carnivores include snakes, tigers and birds of prey such as eagles. Insects, fish, birds, alligators and crocodiles are found in the rivers.

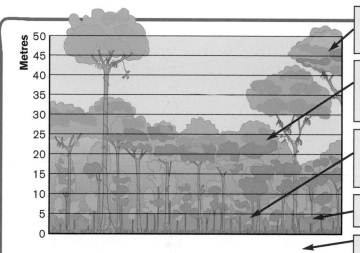

Forest layers

Emergents or forest giants, 50 metres or taller, e.g. kapok. These trees are usually supported by buttress roots

The **canopy** is a dense layer forming almost complete cover. Trees 20–30 metres tall include many hardwoods such as mahogany

The **understorey** is between the canopy and forest floor. This dark, dank area contains saplings between the trunks of larger trees

Large numbers of creepers and lianas entwine themselves around the tree trunks

The **forest floor** is covered in a deep litter of fallen leaves and branches

Destruction of the rainforest

The world's rainforests are being destroyed. No-one knows exactly how fast they are disappearing but some estimates suggest about 40 hectares of rainforest are lost every minute and an area equivalent to five times the size of Switzerland is lost every year. The removal of trees on a large scale is called **deforestation**.

The **timber industry** is responsible for about 40% of forest destruction. Commercial logging provides important income for many LEDC countries. Mechanisation has led to more rapid felling of trees and to widespread destruction as vehicles and machinery drive a way through the forest.

Roads open the way for migrant **subsistence farmers** to come and clear the forest by burning. After 3 or 4 years of farming the infertile soils are exhausted and another patch of forest is cleared. This 'slash and burn' agriculture is a huge threat to forests.

Cattle ranching has a reputation for destroying rainforest to make way for grazing land. The pasture only lasts about 10 years as overgrazing and the torrential rains turn the land into semi-desert.

Large-scale projects, such as iron-ore mining at Carajas in Amazonia, or massive hydroelectric schemes like the Tucuri Dam in Brazil also lead to destruction of the rainforest.

Effects of rainforest deforestation

Deforestation

Change in biodiversity
Removal of the forest causes loss of plant species. Animals are forced out as their food supply and habitat are destroyed. Many rainforest species have become extinct and others are threatened because of loss of habitat

Change in hydrology
Without trees the water cycle is disrupted. Interception and transpiration are both reduced and surface runoff increases. Water and silt pour into rivers, making them flood

Change in soils
Without trees to protect it the soil is easily eroded. Torrential rain removes nutrients via surface runoff and leaching, and the soil becomes infertile. Surface runoff on steep slopes can cause gulleying and mud slides

Change in climate
Transpiration is reduced and evaporation increases. This leads to a drier climate. Deforestation contributes to global warming because trees use up carbon dioxide during photosynthesis. Less forest means there is more carbon dioxide in the atmosphere, and this leads to global warming

Sustainable development

Exploitation of resources such as tropical rainforests is leading to destruction of the ecosystem. In the future the forests will not be able to support local people.

Sustainable development means using resources in a way that will allow continued use in the future. It means being careful with the world's natural resources and ecosystems but still enabling some development to take place.

National Parks

Some countries have set up **National Parks** to protect their rainforests. Examples are the Jau Rainforest Park in Brazil, which is the size of Israel and the largest National Park in the world, and the Korup National Park in the Republic of Cameroon. These areas are protected from development, the aim being to ensure the survival of their unique flora and fauna.

Sustainable logging in Peru

Small-scale schemes to produce timber in a way which does not destroy the forest are in place in the Amazon Basin and in the Solomon Islands. One scheme in Peru involves cutting a strip of forest only 20 metres wide. Portable saws are used to cut the felled trees into logs which can then be transported out of the forest using a cart pulled by oxen. This causes minimum damage to the surrounding forest. The felled area is left to regenerate naturally as seedlings from the surrounding forest spread there. No more felling occurs for up to 40 years.

People in MEDCs can help by making sure that any furniture or wood they buy is from a forest where sustainable methods are used. Most products in this country are now marked to show customers if the wood is produced in this way.

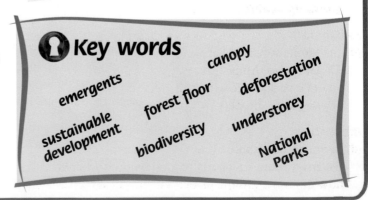

🔑 **Key words**

emergents

canopy

forest floor

deforestation

sustainable development

biodiversity

understorey

National Parks

Test yourself

1 Make a copy of the diagram and label it carefully.

2 Explain why the tropical rainforest is home to such a huge variety of plants and animals.

3 True or false:
   ◆ Tropical rainforest soils are very fertile.
   ◆ Deforestation can disrupt the water cycle.
   ◆ Humus is inorganic.
   ◆ Leaching can remove nutrients from the soil.

Examination question

(a) Where in the cycle is carbon stored
   (i) as a gas
   (ii) as a solid? (2 marks)

(b) Name two ways carbon gets into plant tissues. (2 marks)

(c) What will happen to the carbon if the trees are
   (i) chopped down and burnt
   (ii) chopped down and left to rot while the forest grows up again? (4 marks)

Foundation tier:
(d) (i) Name an ecosystem.
   (ii) Describe the plants and animals that are found in this ecosystem.
   (iii) Say how the ecosystem is used by people. (8 marks)

Higher tier:
(d) Name an ecosystem you have studied, describe the main features of the ecosystem and explain how different groups of people have altered it. (8 marks)

The carbon cycle in a forest ecosystem

Carbon dioxide in the atmosphere

Some carbon dioxide released by plants (through respiration)

Carbon dioxide used in photosynthesis

Some carbon dioxide dissolved in rainwater

Dead leaves and twigs containing carbon fall to ground

Carbon released as leaves and twigs decompose

Carbon dissolved in soil water is taken up by plant roots

🔺 Exam tip

'Name an ecosystem' does not mean 'name an area'. Choose 'tropical rainforest', not 'Amazon basin'.

Distribution of population

People are not evenly distributed over the Earth's surface. This is due to both physical and human factors.

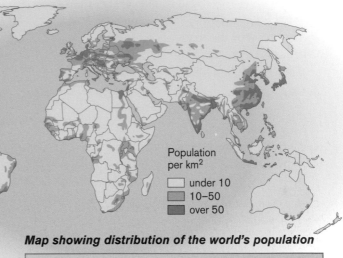

Density of population is measured as the number of people per square kilometre. **Densely-populated** areas have a large number of people per square kilometre. **Sparsely-populated** areas have a small number of people per square kilometre.

Note that most countries have both sparsely and densely-populated areas. In the UK, examples are the sparsely-populated Highlands of Scotland and the densely-populated southeast England.

If there are too many people living in an area for the resources available then the area is **overpopulated**.

If there are too few people to use the resources available fully then the area is **underpopulated**.

Population per km²

- under 10
- 10–50
- over 50

Map showing distribution of the world's population

Sparsely populated	
70% of the Earth's surface is sea	• too dry, e.g. Sahara Desert • too mountainous, e.g. Himalayas
Hostile environments: • too cold, e.g. Arctic Canada	It is difficult to grow crops and keep animals, and life is uncomfortable

Densely populated	
Areas with agreeable climates, e.g. California and Europe	Industrial areas where there is work, e.g. Japan, Europe, northeast USA
Areas rich in natural resources such as coal, oil, gas and metal ores, e.g. Europe	Fertile lowlands with sheltered valleys for growing crops, e.g. Ganges valley, southeast Asia

Population growth

- ◆ The world's population is growing rapidly.
- ◆ It took all of human history until around 1650 to reach the first billion.
- ◆ The second billion took 200 years and the third billion took 70 years.
- ◆ In 13 years, from 1987 to 2000, the population grew from 5 billion to 6 billion.
- ◆ The latest prediction from **demographers** — the people who study population — is that the world population will level off at 9–12 billion around 2070.

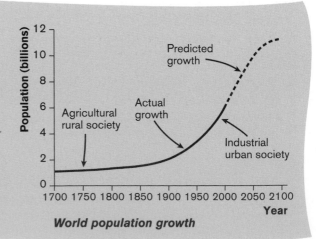

World population growth

The demographic transition model

The demographic transition model shows how the growth of population changes. Population growth is a balance between the number of live babies born and the number of people dying.

Birth rate is the number of live babies born per 1,000 of the population each year.

Death rate is the number of deaths per 1,000 of the population each year.

Natural increase is the difference between the birth rate and the death rate. If the birth rate is high and the death rate is low then the population will increase naturally.

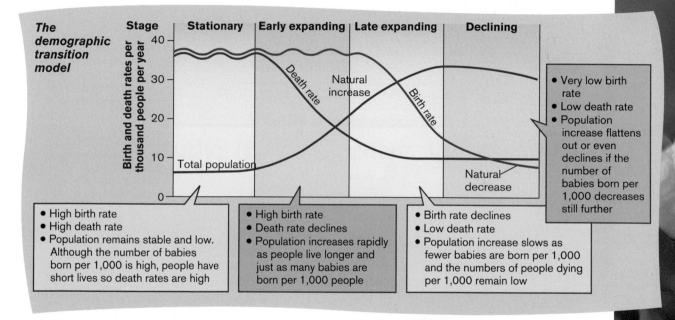

The demographic transition model

| Stage | Stationary | Early expanding | Late expanding | Declining |

Birth and death rates per thousand people per year

Death rate · Natural increase · Birth rate · Total population · Natural decrease

- High birth rate
- High death rate
- Population remains stable and low. Although the number of babies born per 1,000 is high, people have short lives so death rates are high

- High birth rate
- Death rate declines
- Population increases rapidly as people live longer and just as many babies are born per 1,000 people

- Birth rate declines
- Low death rate
- Population increase slows as fewer babies are born per 1,000 and the numbers of people dying per 1,000 remain low

- Very low birth rate
- Low death rate
- Population increase flattens out or even declines if the number of babies born per 1,000 decreases still further

Changing population growth

In some countries, such as Italy and Portugal, the population is **declining** and in many MEDCs, including the UK, the rate of growth is very slow.

In some countries, particularly LEDCs in Africa and Asia, populations are still **increasing** rapidly.

Smaller families ← **Declining population** → Higher female literacy rates give women more opportunities

Greater use of contraception ← **Declining population** → Women marrying later and having careers

Large families ← **Increasing population** → Slowing death rate as diseases are controlled

Lack of contraception ← **Increasing population** → Early marriage so long period of child-bearing

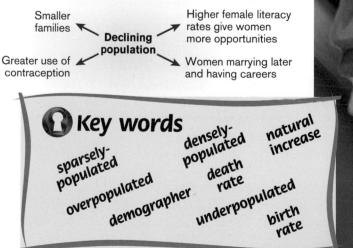

🔑 Key words

sparsely-populated · densely-populated · natural increase · overpopulated · demographer · death rate · underpopulated · birth rate

GCSE Geography

Population structure

Population structure is shown as a **population pyramid** — which is like two bar graphs back to back, one for males and one for females.

Life expectancy is how long on average people can expect to live.

Infant mortality is the number of babies who die under the age of 5 years per 1,000 people.

Economically active are people in work.

Young dependants are children under 15 years old who are dependent on older economically-active people for their needs.

Elderly dependants are people, usually over 60, who are dependent on younger economically-active people.

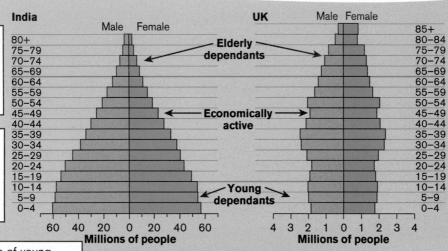

Few elderly dependants as life expectancy is relatively low

Narrowing pyramid as death rate remains relatively high

Large numbers of young dependants as birth rate is high, but this declines rapidly as infant mortality is high

High number of elderly dependants. More females than males as females have longer life expectancy

Rectangular shape as most babies born live to middle and old age

Declining number of births as families are becoming smaller

Population pyramids for India (a typical LEDC) and the UK (a typical MEDC) in 2000

Case study: China's one-child policy

◆ China has the world's largest population at 1,250 billion.
◆ In 1970 the Chinese government aimed to reduce the population growth rate to zero by 2000.
◆ Families are allowed only one child and are fined if they have more.
◆ Rewards include free education, guaranteed jobs, loans.
◆ Birth rates fell from 33 per 1,000 to 16 per 1,000.
◆ Population growth is slowing down.
◆ Policy condemned by many and now relaxed to two children.
◆ 'Missing girls': there are fewer girls than boys registered at birth. Families can have only one child and want a son. What happens to the girls?

Population pyramids are used to help predict changes in the population and plan for the future. They can be used to predict the proportion of elderly people in the population who will need health care, or the number of young people who will be economically active in the future.

Migration

Migration is the movement of people from one region or country to another.

Emigration is people (emigrants) leaving a region or country.

Immigration is people (immigrants) entering a region or country.

Why do people move?

Push factors (cause people to leave)
- low wages so low standard of living
- lack of job opportunities
- poor quality of life
- lack of amenities, e.g. hospitals, schools
- conflict, e.g. civil war, oppression
- natural hazard, e.g. volcano, drought

Pull factors (attract people to an area)
- high wages and improved standard of living
- improved job opportunities, promotion
- better amenities and services
- improved quality of life
- better environment, no natural hazards
- freedom from oppression

Rural
Poverty, lack of opportunity, no secondary schools. Young, skilled and able people leave. The elderly, female, less able and sick are left behind, leading to greater inefficiency in farming, and more poverty

Urban
Growing number of new arrivals in the city increases pressure on already limited opportunities. Shortage of housing means people live in poor conditions. Lack of regular paid work leads to crime and poverty

---

 ## Case study: Mexican migration to USA

- People want to cross the border from Mexico to the USA.
- GNP per capita in the USA is $26,980, and in Mexico is $3,320.
- Most migrants are looking for better jobs, better pay and improved standards of living.
- An estimated 5 million Mexicans are living in the USA.
- Some legal migrants are seasonal workers, e.g. harvesting the summer crops.

- It is estimated that up to 1 million Mexicans try to enter the USA each year. Many are caught crossing the border and sent back.
- Most migrants are young men. The older people are left at home so the economically-active population declines.
- At one time migration was encouraged so migrants could do low-paid and dirty jobs. US workers saw migrants as a threat to jobs and a drain on resources.

🔒 Key words

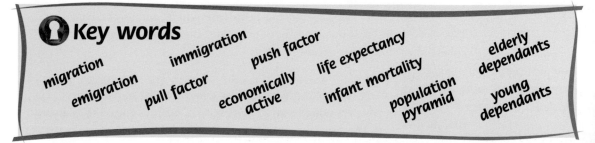

migration   immigration   push factor   life expectancy   elderly dependants

emigration   pull factor   economically active   infant mortality   population pyramid   young dependants

Test yourself

1 Cross out the incorrect word(s) from those in italic in the following.

(a) Sparsely-populated areas are *too cold*, *too flat*, *too dry*, and *too mountainous* to live in.

(b) Densely-populated areas are *industrial*, *rich in natural resources* or *infertile plateaus*.

(c) Overpopulated areas have *too few/too many people* for the resources available.

(d) Birth rate is the number of live babies born *per 100/1,000/10,000* of the population each *month/year*.

2 Complete the sentences.

(a) In the early expanding stage of the transition model the death rate is…

(b) Two features of the late expanding stage of the demographic model are…

(c) Three features of a population pyramid are…

(d) Three reasons why population growth declines are…

(e) Five push factors causing people to migrate are…

Examination question

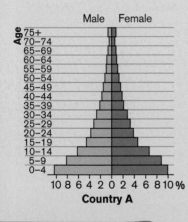

Country A

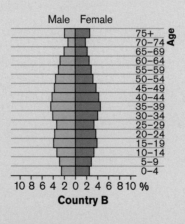

Country B

(a) Look at the diagram which shows population pyramids for two countries, A and B. One is an LEDC and the other an MEDC.

(i) Which of the two pyramids is for an LEDC?

(1 mark)

(ii) Explain how changes in the death rate may affect the size of the population. (2 marks)

(iii) What planning problems might result in a country with a population structure similar to that of country A? (4 marks)

(vi) Why has the rate of population growth in some countries declined? (4 marks)

Foundation tier:

(b) Describe some of the problems which may be caused, in both the area they leave and the area they move to, when people migrate. (6 marks)

Higher tier:

(b) Using one or more examples describe and explain the problems which may be caused, in both the area they leave and the area they move to, when people migrate. (6 marks)

🔺 Exam tip

Command words like 'describe' and 'explain' are very important (explain is the same as asking for reasons). Notice in the last question that the examiner asks you to use examples from your case-study knowledge.

Settlement

A **settlement** is a place where people live. It can be a single house but is more usually a group of houses. It can be any size from a small hamlet of a few buildings to a large city.

Choosing a site

The place where a settlement is built is known as its **site**. The site of a settlement is chosen for a reason. Most settlements in the UK are hundreds of years old, and the site was chosen for reasons which suited needs at that time.

The top diagram shows the main reasons for choosing a site. In reality there were often several reasons for choosing a site.

Sketch map to show the situation of London

Choosing the site for a settlement

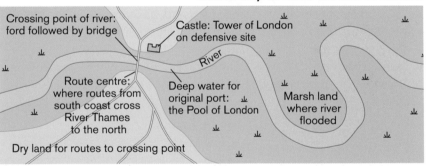

5 Good building materials: wood and stone. Wood also used for fuel

6 Where resources can easily be exploited

7 Easy access to other settlements at crossing point of river

Surrounding hills shelter the valley

4 Good farmland for food supply, sheltered valley

Rock and stone

Woods

Good farmland

Lead mining

Dry ground

Spring

2 Dry land to build on – not marshy

3 Hilltop is easy to defend and away from flooding

1 Good water supply

Stream

Major routeway

Marsh

River

Sketch map to show the site of London

Crossing point of river: ford followed by bridge

Castle: Tower of London on defensive site

River

Route centre: where routes from south coast cross River Thames to the north

Deep water for original port: the Pool of London

Marsh land where river flooded

Dry land for routes to crossing point

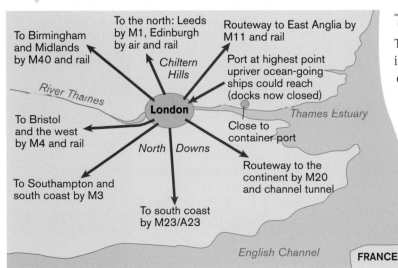

To the north: Leeds by M1, Edinburgh by air and rail

Routeway to East Anglia by M11 and rail

To Birmingham and Midlands by M40 and rail

Chiltern Hills

Port at highest point upriver ocean-going ships could reach (docks now closed)

River Thames

London

Thames Estuary

To Bristol and the west by M4 and rail

Close to container port

North Downs

To Southampton and south coast by M3

Routeway to the continent by M20 and channel tunnel

To south coast by M23/A23

English Channel

FRANCE

The situation

The **situation** of a settlement is its position in relation to other towns or cities, route-ways (road and rail) and physical features such as the coast, hills and mountains, or major rivers.

🔑 **Key words**

situation   site   settlement

GCSE Geography

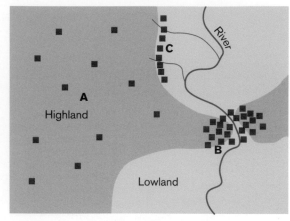

Dispersed, nucleated and linear settlements

Dispersed or nucleated

Maps show that settlements in an area are often arranged in patterns. The three most common are:

Dispersed Spread out, e.g. in highland areas where population is sparse (A).

Nucleated Clustered together around a central point on the map, e.g. a crossing point of a river (B).

Linear Arranged in a line, often at the foot of hills, on the edge of a floodplain, or along a routeway (C).

Settlement hierarchy

Geographers classify settlements in terms of size and the range of services they offer. This is known as the settlement **hierarchy**.

◆ The size of settlements increases the higher up the hierarchy they are, e.g. the small town is larger than the village, and the conurbation is the largest type of settlement.

◆ The number of settlements decreases the higher up the hierarchy they are, e.g. there is a much larger number of villages than towns and very few conurbations.

◆ The number of services which settlements have increases the higher up the hierarchy they are, e.g. a city will have hospitals and department stores but a small town will not have these services.

◆ A **conurbation** exists where one large city has grown to 'swallow up' several surrounding towns or where several large towns or cities have grown together to make one very large built-up area.

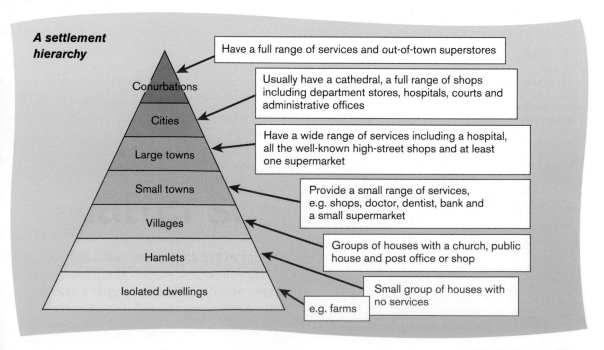

A settlement hierarchy

Conurbations — Have a full range of services and out-of-town superstores

Cities — Usually have a cathedral, a full range of shops including department stores, hospitals, courts and administrative offices

Large towns — Have a wide range of services including a hospital, all the well-known high-street shops and at least one supermarket

Small towns — Provide a small range of services, e.g. shops, doctor, dentist, bank and a small supermarket

Villages — Groups of houses with a church, public house and post office or shop

Hamlets — Small group of houses with no services

Isolated dwellings — e.g. farms

The function of a settlement

The **function** of a settlement is its purpose, for example a port, tourist resort, market town or capital city.

Changing functions

Towns and cities often have more than one function. Oxford is well known as a university town, but also has an important administrative function for the county of Oxfordshire, and an industrial function making motor cars.

The main function of a town may change. This is true of some coastal towns which were originally fishing ports but are now mainly holiday resorts.

Administrative centre
A place from which areas are governed – county towns or capital cities

Industrial town
A place where goods are made such as iron and steel, cars and textiles or where resources are mined such as coal

Dormitory towns
A town where many inhabitants work elsewhere, usually a big city. They only come to the town at weekends and to sleep

Market town
A central place where goods may be bought and sold and a regular market is held

Function of a settlement

Retirement town
A place where people move to live on retirement, e.g. coastal towns, particularly in southern England, or areas of outstanding beauty

Port
Coastal town on a bay or estuary, importing and exporting goods, or a fishing port

University town
Where the university dominates the town

Holiday resort
Often developed from a small port, with a beach or attractive scenery

Function of a settlement

Case study: Padstow, North Cornwall

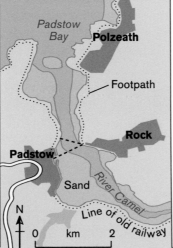

In the past
A small fishing port and harbour
• Ships from Padstow Harbour once sailed to Scandinavia and Canada
• The Camel River was once navigable for 12 km upriver, to Wadebridge
• Padstow Harbour was a busy fishing port
• Streets near the harbour had ship repair yards, sail makers and markets
• The railway took fish to markets in the big cities

Padstow Bay — Polzeath
— Footpath
Rock
Padstow
Sand
River Camel
Line of old railway
N
0   km   2

Today
Mainly a tourist resort
• Pleasure craft outnumber fishing boats
• Only small boats can reach Padstow because the estuary is silted up
• Dredgers take sand from the estuary for use in the building trade
• Sandy beaches and spectacular cliff walks attract hundreds of tourists in the summer
• The disused railway line is now a cycle trail
• Gift shops and cafés crowd the streets near the harbour

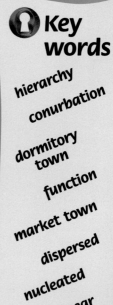

Key words

hierarchy
conurbation
dormitory town
function
market town
dispersed
nucleated
linear

Counter-urbanisation

During the last 20 or 30 years many cities in MEDCs have actually lost population. People and businesses have moved away from large urban centres to small towns or villages. This process is known as **counter-urbanisation**. People move out of large cities for a number of reasons or push factors and are attracted to villages or small towns by pull factors.

Some villages and country towns have grown very rapidly in the last 30 years through **urban–rural migration**. New houses have been built and older ones renovated. In some places the total population has more than doubled, bringing with it great changes to the village, some good and some not so good.

I'd prefer my children to grow up in the countryside. It's cleaner and safer

There's a good road and a rail service from here so we can easily get to the city if we want to

We didn't want to spend our retirement in the city

It's expensive in the city. House prices are high, especially in the nicer areas

The schools in the city were not what I wanted for my children

The city is too busy and noisy. There are endless traffic jams and there is nowhere to park

We've bought a nice house with a garden and we can walk to the shops or out into the countryside

I moved my business because I found an office with a good view and easy access. So much of our work is done by e-mail, fax and telephone that it doesn't really matter where our office is

Counter-urbanisation: push and pull factors

Benefits of counter-urbanisation

✔ There are more people in the village to support local shops, bus services and the village school.

✔ Many old or derelict buildings have been renovated.

✔ There are opportunities for local businesses such as builders, shops, the garage or the pub, and jobs are created locally.

✔ Younger people will settle in the village, creating a more balanced population structure.

Problems caused by counter-urbanisation

✘ House prices go up, making it difficult for local people to buy a house.

✘ Open space is built on and in some cases green belt land has been lost.

✘ There are more cars, causing traffic and parking problems and creating a risk for pedestrians.

✘ Tensions may develop between the older residents of the village and the newcomers.

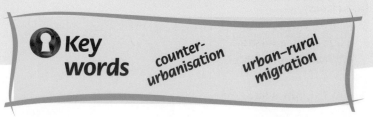

🔑 **Key words** counter-urbanisation urban–rural migration

Test yourself

1 Look at the map. Would you build a settlement at A, B, C or D? Give four reasons for your answer.

2 What is the difference between dispersed and nucleated settlements?

3 List six functions of a settlement.

4 Give two differences between services offered in a city and those in a small town.

5 (a) Give four reasons why people would move from a city to a country village.

(b) Give four effects of people moving from the city to a country village.

Map labels:
Rich well drained soil — A
Good grazing for animals
Marshland
Steep slope to river
Highland no water
B
C
D
Woodland

Exam tip

If there is a graph in the question, make sure you know what the axes represent, and look for general trends and unusual points.

Examination question

(a) Look at the diagram which shows the size and services of some places in East Anglia.

(i) What is meant by services? (1 mark)

(ii) Which place named on the graph has the most services? (1 mark)

(iii) What does the graph show about these places in East Anglia? (2 marks)

Size and services of some places in East Anglia

Increase in number of services (vertical axis)

Increase in size (horizontal axis)

Norwich
Dereham
Attleborough
Claxton

Foundation tier:

(b) (i) What is meant by counter-urbanisation? (1 mark)

(ii) Give four reasons why people move to the countryside from the cities. (4 marks)

(iii) Describe the effects on a village of people moving there from the city. (5 marks)

Higher tier:

(b) For an example of a village you have studied which has grown owing to counter-urbanisation:

(i) Name the village.

(ii) Explain why people have moved from the city to the village.

(iii) Explain what effect this has had on the village. (10 marks)

Land use in MEDC cities

Land use in a city falls into these categories:

Residential Land used for housing.

Industrial Land used for factories and other industrial buildings.

Open space Land used for parks and playgrounds, and derelict or unused land.

Commercial Land used for shops, offices, banks and other businesses.

The diagram shows a model city or the typical layout of land use in an MEDC city. This model is a useful tool, but remember that every town or city is unique. Towns and cities may show similarities to the model city but nowhere will be arranged just like the model.

You may have studied other models such as Hoyt's sector model and Burgess's concentric ring model.

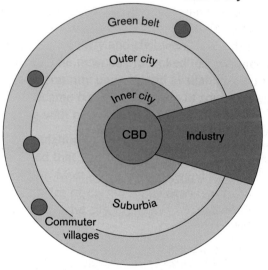

The model city – land use in an MEDC city

Hoyt's sector model of land use

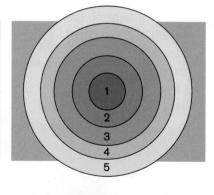

Burgess's concentric model of land use

Key
1 Central business district
2 Manufacturing industry
3 Low-class residential
4 Medium-class residential
5 High-class residential

The city skyline

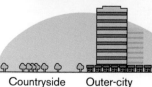

Countryside | Outer-city council estate | Old industrial zone: some old terraced houses and high-rise redevelopment | City centre: large shops, offices and entertainments | Inner city: nineteenth-century terraced houses | Outer city: suburbia. Detached and semi-detached houses | Green belt

The central business district (CBD)

The CBD is at the heart of the city. It is dominated by high-rise buildings occupied by shops, offices, banks and other **commercial functions**. There are often **leisure facilities** such as theatres, cinemas, night clubs, restaurants and pubs, and these may be **clustered** together in a **quarter**. All these functions group together in the CBD because it is the most **accessible** part of the city. People from all over the city and beyond can reach it easily. This pushes up the value of the land and also explains why there are so many high-rise buildings. The high cost of rents in the CBD means that some land uses are not found here, such as housing, industry and large areas of open space.

The magnetic effect of the CBD attracts new shops, clubs, bars and offices.

Accessibility: it is easy for customers and employees to reach the business

Some businesses benefit from locating near similar businesses, e.g. entertainments and comparison shops

Prestige: a central address can help attract custom

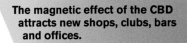

Pull factors

Push factors

Push and pull factors affecting functions in the CBD

But its problems push some functions away from the city centre towards the outskirts.

Very little room for expansion

Land prices are high

Traffic **congestion**, noise and pollution

Local government planning restrictions can restrict development

The changing city centre

The CBD is always changing.
Changes include:
- new buildings
- shopping malls
- public open spaces
- conversion of old buildings for a new use
- pedestrianised areas and one-way streets
- new types of transport such as trams
  (e.g. Manchester and Sheffield)

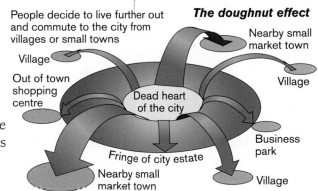

People decide to live further out and commute to the city from villages or small towns

The doughnut effect

Village

Nearby small market town

Out of town shopping centre

Dead heart of the city

Village

Business park

Fringe of city estate

Nearby small market town

Village

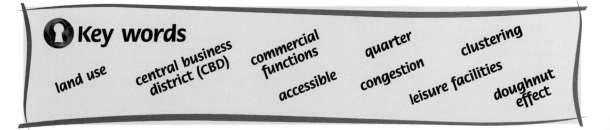

🔑 Key words

land use   central business district (CBD)   commercial functions   accessible   quarter   congestion   clustering   leisure facilities   doughnut effect

The inner city

Most inner-city areas lie close to the CBD and to industrial parts of the city. The inner city is an area of poor-quality, often **nineteenth-century terraced housing**. In the 1960s some of these old terraces were cleared as part of **urban redevelopment schemes** and replaced with council estates including **high-rise flats**. Today many inner-city estates are run down even though they are only about 40 years old.

Inner-city housing

High-rise flats built in the 1960s

Terraced houses built over 100 years ago. Some have become run down

High-density housing and little open space

Parking is often a problem

Why people leave inner-city areas

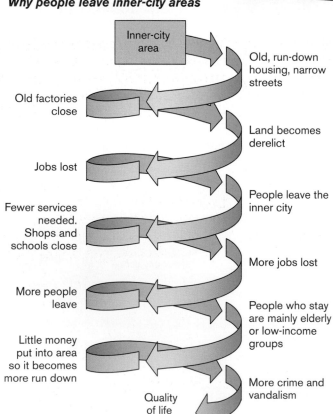

Inner-city area

Old, run-down housing, narrow streets

Old factories close

Land becomes derelict

Jobs lost

People leave the inner city

Fewer services needed. Shops and schools close

More jobs lost

More people leave

People who stay are mainly elderly or low-income groups

Little money put into area so it becomes more run down

More crime and vandalism

Quality of life gets worse

People of the inner city

Many different types of people live in inner-city areas but certain groups are found in quite high numbers:

- ◆ low-income families such as single parents, low-paid manual workers or unemployed people
- ◆ older people living on a state pension
- ◆ black or Asian families
- ◆ newcomers to the city such as students and migrants

Census statistics indicate which groups of people predominate in each ward (voting area) of the city. We call this the **socioeconomic characteristics** of the area.

People living in inner-city areas may have a low **quality of life** because of low incomes, poor-quality housing and inadequate social facilities.

Improving the inner city

Many inner-city areas have undergone huge changes during the last few years, and quality of life for people has begun to improve. Central government pays for the biggest schemes through funds such as SRB (Single Regeneration Budget), and from European funds. Without government help, local councils can only afford small-scale schemes.

Industries move out

When factories and businesses were located in the inner city, local people could find work within easy reach of their homes. Today many of the old factories have closed down because manufacturing has declined. Others have moved away to the outskirts of the city where land is cheaper, there is more space to expand and access to motorways is easier. The narrow streets of the inner city are not attractive to new businesses. This is one of the reasons for high unemployment rates in these areas.

Newly-built flats replacing some terraced housing

Cul-de-sac provides parking space

Street lights increase safety

Old terraced houses renovated and improved

Trees planted to improve environment

Street paved and closed to vehicles

Improved inner city

The census

Every 10 years the British government conducts a census or count. Each household in the country must complete a form which asks questions about the house and the people who live there. For example, everyone has to provide information about their qualifications, their job and whether or not they have a car. The census provides useful information to the government which can be used in planning. It was last completed in April 2000.

🔒 Key words

inner city   urban redevelopment scheme   quality of life   high-rise flats   socioeconomic characteristics   nineteenth-century terraced housing   high-density housing

The outer city

Since the beginning of the twentieth century, cities have spread outwards rapidly. Transport in the form of trams, then buses and much later cars meant that people could live further away from their place of work. It led to the growth of the outer city or **suburbs**.

If you are writing about a suburban area in an exam, use a named area from a town or city you have studied.

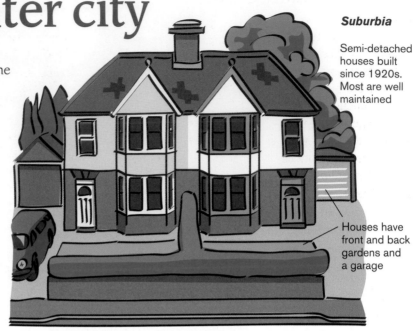

Suburbia

Semi-detached houses built since 1920s. Most are well maintained

Houses have front and back gardens and a garage

There are many different types of houses in the suburbs, including **detached** and **semi-detached houses**, bungalows and flats. The houses are built at lower densities than in the inner city, more of them have gardens and there are more parks and other areas of public open space. There is a huge variety of housing because:
◆ different people need, and can afford, different sorts of houses
◆ building styles have changed enormously during the last 100 years

Living in suburbia

This area is very convenient. There are some good local shops and a nice park where I can take my children

We live in a 1930s semi-detached house. It's a lovely family house with a nice garden

The streets here are well kept with grass verges and all the houses have their own garages

We live in a new house and I can see the country-side from the windows upstairs

Our school has a big field all round it. I can walk to school but lots of my friends come on the bus

Areas of the outer city which have mostly owner-occupied houses are called **suburbia**, but there are also large areas of council housing in the outer city.

Outer-city council estates

Many British cities have large, carefully-planned estates on the outskirts of the city. These were built by local councils in the 1960s when there was a huge demand for new housing. Councils decided to build on **greenfield sites**, because there was not enough space in inner cities. The estates usually have a shopping centre, pub, play area and sometimes a school as well as a variety of housing including high-rise and low-rise flats and modern terraces called town houses.

Outer-city council estate

Nearby school and shopping centre

High-rise flats

Plenty of trees and greenery

Modern terraced houses called town houses

Maisonettes

Bus links to city centre

Living in an outer-city council estate

I feel isolated out here. It's a long way from where I was born and brought up but the council pulled our houses down and I had to move out here

I want to go to town in the evening to meet my friends and go out to a club, but the buses don't go that often and if I get a taxi back home it's very expensive

There's a small shopping centre here but there's not much choice. I like to go into town to do most of my shopping

I really like it here. There are plenty of families and it's safe for the children to play outside. There are good schools nearby and a doctor's surgery close to the shops. It's a friendly estate

I like living out here close to the country-side. There's a lovely view from my flat

🔒 Key words

suburbia   suburbs   outer-city council estate   detached houses   semi-detached houses   greenfield site

Services in the city

All towns and cities provide a range of services for local people. These include medical services, shops, leisure facilities, education and public transport. Some groups of people have better access to services than others and this can affect quality of life.

Shopping centres in a town

The diagram shows that most towns have:

One major shopping centre in the CBD which contains the largest shops such as department stores and chain stores. These need lots of customers to support them (they have a **high threshold**) and so they locate in the most accessible part of the city. The shops may sell **high-order goods**, such as expensive clothes, electrical equipment and furniture.

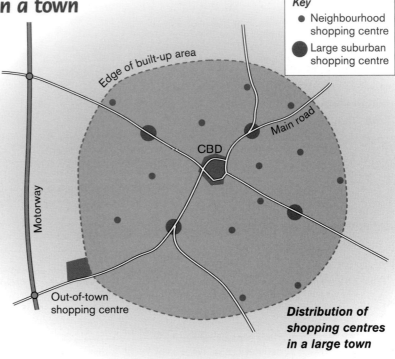

Key
- ● Neighbourhood shopping centre
- ● Large suburban shopping centre

Distribution of shopping centres in a large town

Several large suburban shopping centres, usually located towards the centre of the city at major road junctions. These locations provide good access from surrounding residential areas. As well as supermarkets and other food shops there will be banks, estate agents, charity shops and hardware stores.

Many neighbourhood shopping centres with anywhere between six and 60 shops. They will mostly sell **low-order goods** and services such as food, newspapers, fish and chips and hairdressing. These shops have a **low threshold** and rely on frequent visits from people living nearby.

Corner shops These used to form an important part of the shopping **hierarchy** but many of them have closed as they are unable to compete with large supermarkets or other businesses which sell cheaply and stay open for long hours.

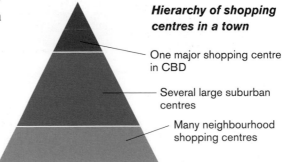

Hierarchy of shopping centres in a town

- One major shopping centre in CBD
- Several large suburban centres
- Many neighbourhood shopping centres

Out-of-town shopping centres

In recent years changes to people's lifestyle have affected shopping patterns:
◆ more people have more money to spend (disposable income)
◆ many more families have a car, giving them access to new shopping centres
◆ electrical appliances such as freezers and microwave ovens mean people buy for several days or weeks in advance and no longer buy fresh food every day
◆ more women work and have less time to shop every day than in the past

Some people are worried that traditional shopping centres will suffer as their customers find it more convenient or cheaper to shop elsewhere.

Today many cities have:
◆ several **superstores** on the outskirts
◆ out-of-town **retail parks** with large electrical stores, carpet warehouses and computer shops
◆ large **out-of-town shopping centres** such as the Metro Centre in Gateshead, the Trafford Centre in Manchester and Meadowhall in Sheffield

These types of retail developments are generally located on the outskirts of a city where land values are lower and there is more space available to build and expand. It is important for them to be close to main roads or motorways so there is easy access for both their customers and delivery vehicles, and away from the congestion of the city centre.

🔍 Case study: Trafford Centre, Manchester

The Manchester area is densely populated. This means there are large numbers of customers for shops in the Trafford Centre. Over 30 million people visit each year

The large population means there is also a large potential workforce. There are full- and part-time jobs available for men and women

The site beside the motorway was in need of redevelopment. There was space to build the large shopping centre and room for expansion in the future

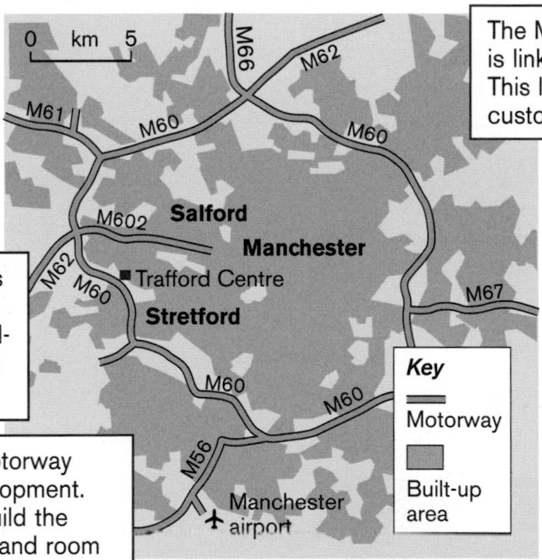

The M60 encircles Manchester and is linked to other major motorways. This location means easy access for customers and deliveries

Most of the shops sell high-order goods and services. They need to attract people from a large catchment area

The centre was opened in 1998. It has over 200 shops and leisure facilities including a multi-screen cinema and restaurants. There are 10,000 free car-parking spaces

Map showing location of Trafford Centre

Map labels: M66, M62, M61, M60, M602, Salford, Manchester, M62, M60, Trafford Centre, Stretford, M67, M60, M60, M56, Manchester airport, 0 km 5

Key
Motorway
Built-up area

🔑 Key words

high threshold   low threshold   high-order goods   low-order goods   superstores   retail parks   out-of-town shopping centres   hierarchy

The green belt

As cities grow they spread out into the surrounding countryside. One way decision-makers try to stop towns taking over the country-side is by creating a **green belt** of undeveloped land around cities. London was the first city to have a green belt (1947) but the map shows that many others have followed suit.

The aims of a green belt are:
◆ to stop **urban sprawl**
◆ to prevent towns and cities merging into each other
◆ to protect the countryside
◆ to encourage development within the town, not around it

Designation of land as green belt does not mean it will never be built on. If a developer can prove that building is needed, green belt land can be used. This happened when the M25 motorway was built round London and when Manchester airport was given permission to expand.

Today the enormous need for new houses means that some areas of green belt land have been built on and others are threatened. Britain needs about 5 million new homes by 2020 and most of these need to be in southeast England. There are not enough **brownfield sites** (land which has been built on before) for all the extra houses, so there is pressure to build on green belt.

Green belts in England and Wales (1986)

Key
▉ Urban area
▨ Green belt

0   km   100

N

Newcastle
Bradford   York
Manchester   Leeds
Liverpool
Sheffield
Stoke-on-Trent
Nottingham
Birmingham   Coventry
Gloucester
Oxford
London
Bristol
Southampton

See p. 58 where there is information about counter-urbanisation.

New housing in the green belt

There is a demand for large detached and semi-detached houses in pleasant surroundings. These houses can fetch a high price

Modern houses have excellent facilities inside and a garage and small garden outside

It is cheaper for developers to build on greenfield sites on the edge of towns than to redevelop brownfield sites in older parts of a town or city

Permission has been given for 10,000 new homes in green belt land west of the town of Stevenage in Hertfordshire, despite huge opposition from environmental groups

🔑 **Key words**

green belt

urban sprawl

brownfield site

Test yourself

Complete this table. Use named examples you have studied.

	Advantages of living in this area	Disadvantages of living in this area	Named example
Inner-city council estate (high-rise flats and maisonettes)			
Outer-city suburban area (detached and semi-detached houses)			
Old inner-city area (nineteenth-century terraced)			
Outer-city council estate			

1 Which of the following are most likely to be found on the outskirts of a city:

new housing estate, old industrial development, small suburban shopping centre, out-of-town shopping centre, hospital, bus station, new industrial development?

2 Why do developers prefer to build on greenfield sites than to redevelop brownfield sites within a built-up area?

Examination question

(a) Read the newspaper article on the right and suggest two reasons why people are moving away from inner-city areas. (2 marks)

(b) In what ways might the quality of life of people living in a small town or village be better than that of people living in inner-city areas? (3 marks)

Foundation tier:

(c) Choose a settlement you have studied which is growing or declining. It could be a village, a town or a city.
(i) Name the settlement and give its location.
(ii) State whether it is growing or declining and give reasons for the change.
(iii) Explain how the change has affected the people who live there. (8 marks)

Higher tier:

(c) Some settlements are growing whilst others are declining. Use examples you have studied to explain the benefits and problems that arise from either settlement growth or decline. (8 marks)

 Exam tip

Read information like this carefully. Use a highlighter pen to mark key points.

60,000 people have moved out of London

A government report published recently showed that 60,000 people have left London during the last 15 years. These figures are part of a national trend which has seen people leaving the cities for the green fields, clean air and lower crime rates of the countryside. There are now more than 1.25 million fewer people living in the UK's major cities compared with 1985. This is an average of 7,500 leaving every month.

World urbanisation

The total population of the world is just over 6 billion. About 45% of these people live in towns or cities, in other words in urban areas. The proportion of people living in rural and urban areas varies in different parts of the world.

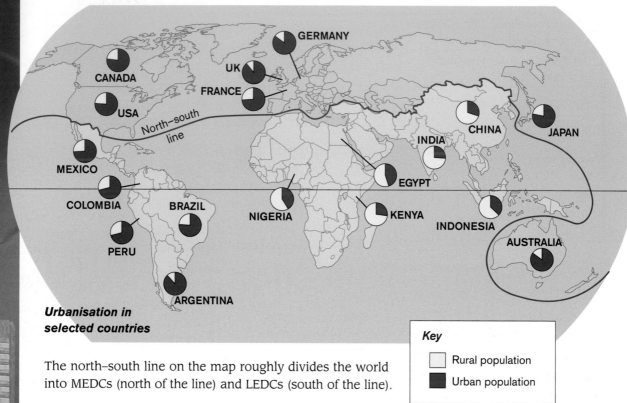

Urbanisation in selected countries

Key

☐ Rural population

■ Urban population

The north–south line on the map roughly divides the world into MEDCs (north of the line) and LEDCs (south of the line).

The proportion of people living in urban areas is much greater in MEDCs, such as France, Japan, Australia, the USA and the UK. Urbanisation occurred in these countries during the nineteenth and twentieth centuries, following the Industrial Revolution. Today most jobs in MEDCs are in manufacturing or service industries, which tend to be based in towns. There are relatively small numbers of farmers, so the rural population is low.

LEDCs usually have a smaller percentage of their populations living in urban areas, but there is a marked difference between countries in South America and those in Africa and Asia. More people live in towns in South America.

MEDCs = more economically developed countries

LEDCs = less economically developed countries

Urbanisation is the increase in the proportion of people who live in towns and cities. It is occurring on a global scale and in most LEDCs. It is no longer taking place in Europe and America.

Urban growth is the expansion of towns and cities so that they cover more land, as well as gaining larger populations.

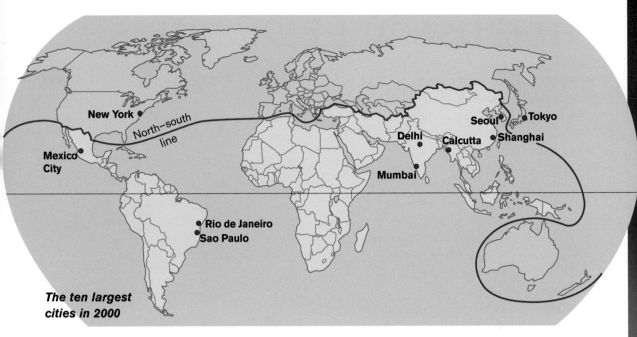

The ten largest cities in 2000

This map shows the ten largest cities in the world. Look at their distribution. Only two of them, Tokyo and New York, are in MEDCs. All the rest are in LEDCs.

All these cities (and about 300 others world-wide) have over one million inhabitants and are known as **millionaire cities**. Cities with over 10 million inhabitants are known as **mega-cities**.

Cities in LEDCs are growing rapidly. This is due to two important processes:

Rural to urban migration The movement of people away from the countryside into towns and cities (see p. 53).

Natural population increase The growth in population because birth rates are higher than death rates. This is common in LEDC cities because many young people but few old people live there.

Rural to urban migration is the result of **push and pull factors**:

Pull factors attract people to the cities:
◆ the hope of work and the chance to make money
◆ better schools
◆ health care
◆ 'bright lights' and entertainment

Push factors encourage people to leave the villages:
◆ poverty
◆ few jobs except in farming
◆ poor health facilities
◆ few schools
◆ little entertainment, especially for young people

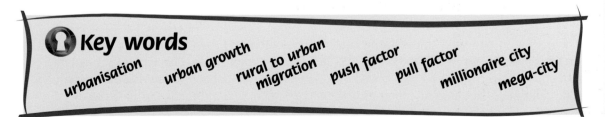

🔒 Key words

urbanisation   urban growth   rural to urban migration   push factor   pull factor   millionaire city   mega-city

Land use in LEDC cities

The pattern of land use in a typical LEDC city is different from that in an MEDC city:

♦ The CBD has high-rise buildings containing offices and shops. This is a busy and often congested area.

♦ Industry usually forms a sector following a river or a main road. Manufacturing industries often include textiles and footwear, bottled drinks and food processing and sometimes car assembly and chemical plants. Many of the factories may be owned by multi-national companies.

♦ High-class housing, especially luxury apartment blocks, is often found close to the city centre. It is convenient for work and shops in a city where moving around may be difficult.

♦ Middle-class housing may merge into the poor but permanent housing, covering quite a large area.

♦ The poorest housing and **squatter settlements** or **shanty towns** surround the city and may cover a large area. Shanty towns may also be found on very steep slopes, land liable to flood or land near to quarries or large factories — in other words land that is really unsuitable for housing.

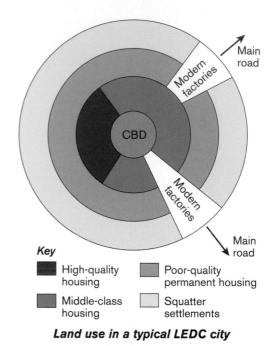

Key

■ High-quality housing
■ Middle-class housing
■ Poor-quality permanent housing
□ Squatter settlements

Land use in a typical LEDC city

Two important things to remember are:

♦ The quality of housing decreases with distance from the city centre. This is the opposite pattern to an MEDC city.

♦ The contrast between wealthy members of society and poor people is very marked in most LEDC cities, and greater than the contrast in MEDC cities.

Shanty towns or squatter settlements

The poorest urban inhabitants live in squatter settlements or shanty towns which grow up on the outskirts of the city and on any derelict land or open space. This type of settlement can cover a large area and may house over 30% of the population. Squatter settlements have different names in different countries, e.g. *bustee* (India), *favela* (Brazil), *barriada* (Peru).

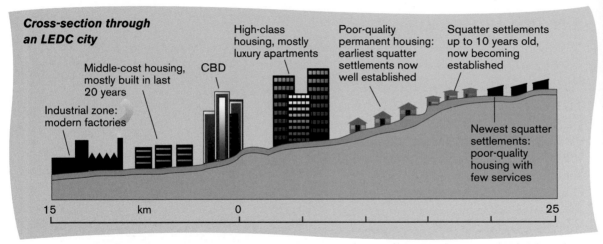

Cross-section through an LEDC city

Industrial zone: modern factories

Middle-cost housing, mostly built in last 20 years

CBD

High-class housing, mostly luxury apartments

Poor-quality permanent housing: earliest squatter settlements now well established

Squatter settlements up to 10 years old, now becoming established

Newest squatter settlements: poor-quality housing with few services

15   km   0   25

Spontaneous squatter settlements are built illegally by very poor people who cannot afford proper housing. They are often newly-arrived migrants from the countryside. The buildings are usually made with locally-available materials, such as mud bricks or wooden walls and plastic or corrugated-iron roofs.

The main problems are:

◆ Very crowded areas with high population densities.
◆ Few basic services such as clean water and sanitation, waste disposal, electricity supplies or paved roads.
◆ Disease is common and there is inadequate health care. There is high infant mortality and a short life expectancy.

◆ There are not enough 'formal' jobs and squatter areas may be a long way from the CBD, so many people earn what they can from informal occupations such as street trading.
◆ The location is often dangerous or unpleasant — next to rubbish tips or quarries or on very steep land prone to landslides.

Tackling the problems of shanty towns

Providing housing for the poor

City authorities are aware of the problems of large squatter settlements but rarely have enough resources to tackle them. In some cities, such as Lagos in Nigeria and Caracas in Venezuela, the authorities have built apartment blocks to re-house people. In most places this is not a practical solution because there is not enough money available.

We were lucky to get this flat. There are thousands of families who need a home and more are arriving every week. There are nowhere near enough flats for everyone who wants one

The flat is nice but it is a long way from the city centre and from where we used to live

My family would rather have a place more like our home in the countryside. We would like to grow a few vegetables and keep chickens

This flat is too expensive for us. I cannot get a factory job and don't earn enough to pay the rent

Site and service schemes

In some countries the authorities have tried to help migrants to the city to build their houses according to careful guidelines. This can be successful if the number of migrants is not too large.

An area of land is found which is not too far from work places in the city. It is divided up by the authorities into individual plots of land. Roads, water and sanitation may be provided. Newcomers can rent a plot of land and build their own house, following certain guidelines. As time goes by and they have more money they can improve their house, for example by making it bigger.

Advantages	Disadvantages
✔ cheaper than building new flats	✘ difficult to provide enough plots of land for the huge numbers needing housing
✔ houses are better built because of guidelines	
✔ water and sanitation supplies reduce risk of disease	✘ families without employment cannot afford rent

This approach was used in Lima in Peru. New townships such as Villa el Salvador were laid out in the desert surrounding the city (see case study on p. 76).

Self-help schemes

Once people have built a house, no matter how basic it is to start with, they are likely to improve it, if and when they can. However, they will only do this if they are confident they will not be thrown off the land. If people are to improve their homes they must therefore be given legal ownership of the land.

Self-help schemes are important in almost all big cities in LEDCs. People improve their houses slowly, for example replacing mud walls with bricks or breeze blocks, and fitting proper windows and doors. The house may gradually be enlarged, building more rooms and then adding upper floors. City authorities will usually provide clean water from standpipes in the street, and later help with sanitation and waste collection. Commercial bus operators will start bus services, and health centres may be built by the local community. In this way people work together to improve their area and over time it changes from a poor, illegal settlement to a legal, medium-quality housing area.

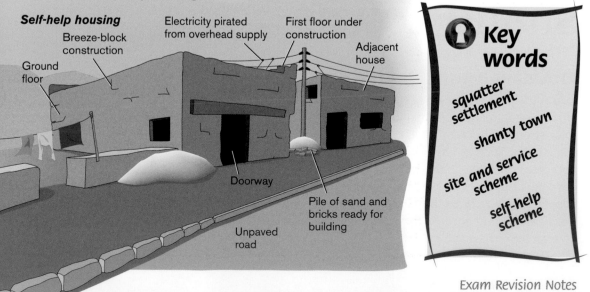

Self-help housing

Breeze-block construction

Electricity pirated from overhead supply

First floor under construction

Adjacent house

Ground floor

Doorway

Pile of sand and bricks ready for building

Unpaved road

🔑 **Key words**

squatter settlement

shanty town

site and service scheme

self-help scheme

Case study: Peru

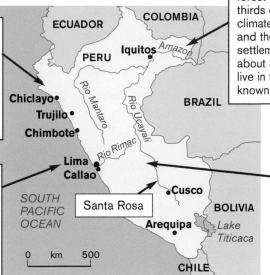

The narrow area of low-lying land along the coast is known as the *costa*. It has a desert climate and lack of rain means settlements must be built on rivers. Fishing is important along the coast

Eastern Peru is part of the Amazon basin. Tropical rainforest covers almost two thirds of the country. The climate is hot and humid and the dense jungle makes settlement difficult. Only about 3% of the population live in this area which is also known as the *selva*

Lima is the capital and much the largest city in Peru, with about 8 million inhabitants. It is built on the Rio Rimac. The port of Callao is now part of Lima

The Andes, which rise to over 6,000 metres above sea level, dominate central Peru. This area is home to Peruvian Indians, direct descendants of the Incas. Many still live in small villages high in the mountains, but numbers are falling as people leave the countryside and migrate to Lima

Living in the Andes in Peru

The Quechua Indians live 3,000 metres up in the Peruvian Andes in villages where there are no shops of any description, and no electricity, gas or running water. They have their own language and this makes their lives difficult in Peru, where most people speak Spanish.

The village of Santa Rosa in the department of Ayacucho, northwest of Cusco, has fewer than 200 inhabitants. Farming is difficult because of the steep slopes and thin soils. The altitude means temperatures are low, especially in winter. Local people grow maize and vegetables such as potatoes, which form their staple diet. They keep sheep, goats and llamas which provide them with milk, cheese and wool.

Their houses are small and made from mud bricks dried in the sun. Families of six or seven may live together in two rooms, cooking on a simple stove or open fire. Water is collected from a standpipe in the village or from a local stream.

There is a school in the neighbouring village about 20 minutes' walk away. Most children leave school when they are 11 or 12. It is a 2-day trek down the treacherous mountainside to get even basic medical care, and common illnesses like diarrhoea or chest and ear infections can easily become life-threatening.

The quality of life here is poor and many young people decide to leave the village in the hope that they can have a better life in the city. Most go to Lima. They leave because of the hardship and lack of opportunities in the village. They may send money back to their families but their departure can cause problems:

◆ Young and better-educated people, especially young men, leave the village.
◆ If too many people leave, local services such as the school are threatened.
◆ Houses and land around the village are deserted and fall into disrepair.
◆ The older people left behind find it hard to manage the farms. Crop yields fall.

Case study: Lima

Lima, the capital of Peru and its largest city, has a population of about 8 million. The city was founded 1535. It has only about 40 mm of rain a year (London has 550 mm). In winter Lima has an almost constant sea mist called *garua*. The city grew on the River Rimac, which was used as a water supply. It also has a port, a commercial centre and a seaside area.

Lima has grown rapidly in the last 40 years. Industry has developed around the port and main roads and many people have moved into the city from the countryside, particularly from villages in the Andes. During the 1970s and 1980s poverty and civil war forced people out of the mountains and thousands arrived in Lima. The newcomers looked for homes and jobs and settled close to roads and factories and on any unused land available. These areas became *barriadas* — areas of squatter housing with many families crowded together.

The population is still growing rapidly and it is estimated that 150,000 people arrive in Lima each year. Most settle on the rugged foothills of the Andes or on the sandy desert lands to the south of the city.

Map of Lima showing location of Villa el Salvador

0   km   10

N

PACIFIC OCEAN

Steep mountains

400 m

River Rimac

Callao (port)

Key
- CBD
- Industry (along main roads and river)
- Other housing areas
- Poorest housing

Area of best housing

Villa el Salvador

Steep mountains

400 m

Semi-desert

Villa el Salvador

In 1971 the city authorities were faced with the massive problem of thousands of squatters on land all around the city centre. They were unable to provide any housing for these people but decided to give them an area of land 25 km to the south of the city centre in the desert. Here a grid of streets was laid out and plots of land were allocated to migrants so they could build their own houses. Today this area, called Villa el Salvador, has a population of over 300,000. It is as large as a city in its own right. This is an example of a **site and service scheme**.

What has the government done?
- provided a clean water supply from standpipes
- built a new sewage disposal system
- installed a supply of electricity
- provided tarmac roads
- installed street lights

What have the people done?
- built their own houses — at first one room, then adding more as time and money allowed
- worked together to set up community facilities such as schools, medical centres and community kitchens to help people feed their families more cheaply
- set up small businesses such as shops, garages, furniture-makers etc.
- established women's cooperative groups making clothes or knitting to help earn money for the family

All these factors have helped improve the quality of life in Villa el Salvador.

Test yourself

1 Give two reasons why cities in LEDCs (for example Lima) are growing very quickly.

2 Explain why the largest cities in MEDCs (for example London) have stable or decreasing populations.

3 Explain why quality of life is low in rural areas in LEDCs (for example in the Peruvian Andes).

4 What are the 'push and pull factors' which cause rural to urban migration?

5 Draw a diagram to show the typical layout of an LEDC city. Label it carefully.

6 Describe and explain the differences in the pattern of land use in cities in LEDC and MEDC countries.

7 What are 'spontaneous settlements'?

8 List four problems of spontaneous settlements.

9 Give three ways in which spontaneous settlements can be improved, and give one advantage and one disadvantage of each.

Examination question

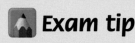 **Exam tip**

Always use figures when answering questions about graphs.

(a) Study the graph. Compare the changes in population shown in Tokyo and Jakarta.

(2 marks)

(b) Suggest reasons for the differences in population growth in the two cities. (4 marks)

(c) Describe the problems that may be created for Jakarta between 1970 and 2015.

(4 marks)

Foundation tier:

(d) Name a town or city where an improvement scheme has taken place.
 ◆ Describe how the area has been improved.
 ◆ Explain how different groups of people were affected by the improvements. (8 marks)

Higher tier:

(d) Name an urban area you have studied. Describe how the area has been improved and explain how successful these improvements have been for different groups of people. (8 marks)

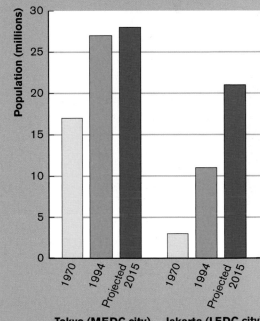

Graph showing population change in Tokyo and Jakarta

Tokyo (MEDC city)   Jakarta (LEDC city)

Farming as a system

The type of farming in an area is influenced by:

Physical factors such as the climate, relief and soils.

Human factors such as the size of the farm and the decisions made by the farmer and governments.

Farms are either **arable** (they grow crops) or **pastoral** (they rear animals). Some **mixed farms** do both.

Input–output model

All farms can be summed up using an input–output model.

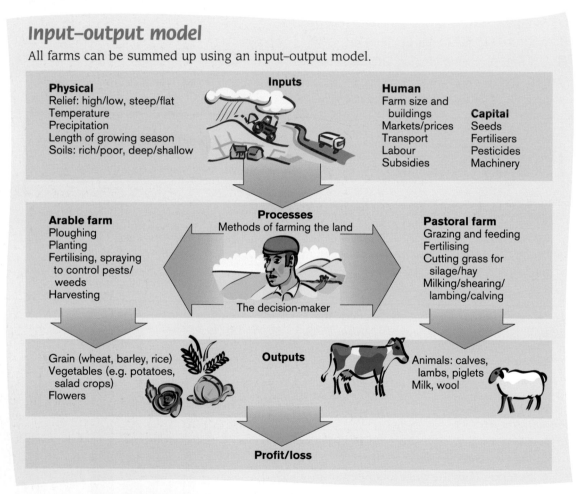

Inputs

Physical
Relief: high/low, steep/flat
Temperature
Precipitation
Length of growing season
Soils: rich/poor, deep/shallow

Human
Farm size and
buildings
Markets/prices
Transport
Labour
Subsidies

Capital
Seeds
Fertilisers
Pesticides
Machinery

Processes
Methods of farming the land

The decision-maker

Arable farm
Ploughing
Planting
Fertilising, spraying
to control pests/
weeds
Harvesting

Pastoral farm
Grazing and feeding
Fertilising
Cutting grass for
silage/hay
Milking/shearing/
lambing/calving

Outputs

Grain (wheat, barley, rice)
Vegetables (e.g. potatoes,
salad crops)
Flowers

Animals: calves,
lambs, piglets
Milk, wool

Profit/loss

Farming classification

Farming may also be classified as:

Intensive Small farms with high inputs of technology, e.g. machinery and fertilisers in European market gardening, or labour in southeast Asian rice farming. The inputs result in high yields per hectare. The most extreme case is factory farming in which animals, such as battery hens, are kept in small pens and crops are grown under controlled conditions (e.g. mushrooms grown on racks in small sheds).

Extensive Very large farms with a low input of technology or labour resulting in low crop yields per hectare (e.g. the wheat farms of North America), or low density of animals per hectare (e.g. the sheep stations of Australia).

Commercial Farms where the animals or crops are produced for sale. This is the case with most farms in the UK.

Subsistence Farms where the crops or animals are reared for consumption by the farmer. Any surplus may be sold at the market.

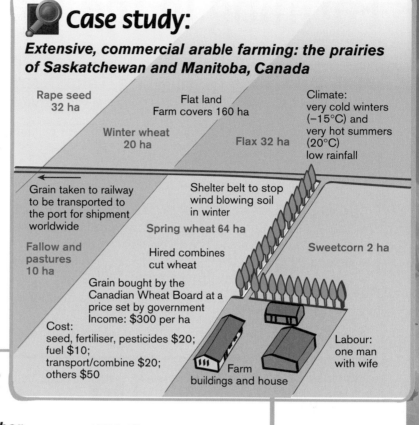

Case study:

Extensive, commercial arable farming: the prairies of Saskatchewan and Manitoba, Canada

Rape seed 32 ha

Flat land Farm covers 160 ha

Winter wheat 20 ha

Flax 32 ha

Climate: very cold winters (−15°C) and very hot summers (20°C) low rainfall

Grain taken to railway to be transported to the port for shipment worldwide

Shelter belt to stop wind blowing soil in winter

Spring wheat 64 ha

Sweetcorn 2 ha

Fallow and pastures 10 ha

Hired combines cut wheat

Grain bought by the Canadian Wheat Board at a price set by government Income: $300 per ha

Cost: seed, fertiliser, pesticides $20; fuel $10; transport/combine $20; others $50

Farm buildings and house

Labour: one man with wife

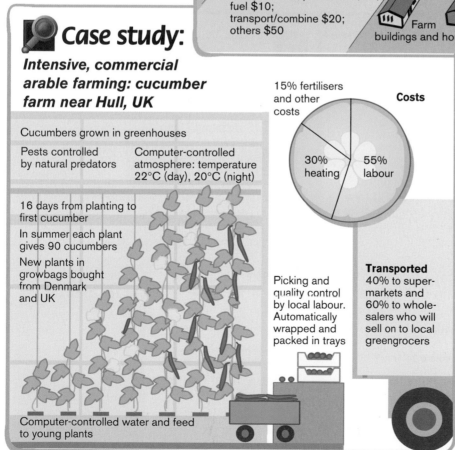

Case study:

Intensive, commercial arable farming: cucumber farm near Hull, UK

Cucumbers grown in greenhouses

Pests controlled by natural predators

Computer-controlled atmosphere: temperature 22°C (day), 20°C (night)

16 days from planting to first cucumber

In summer each plant gives 90 cucumbers

New plants in growbags bought from Denmark and UK

Costs

15% fertilisers and other costs

30% heating

55% labour

Picking and quality control by local labour. Automatically wrapped and packed in trays

Transported 40% to super-markets and 60% to whole-salers who will sell on to local greengrocers

Computer-controlled water and feed to young plants

Key words

inputs

processes

outputs

pastoral farming

arable farming

mixed farming

intensive

extensive

subsistence

GCSE Geography

Farming in the British Isles

A Upland sheep farming, e.g. Lake District hill farm

Area   Mountains and uplands of western Scotland, Wales and northern England

Relief   Rugged hills with steep slopes unsuitable for machinery

Soils   Poor

Climate   Average temperatures: January 6°C, July 15°C. Annual rainfall over 1,000 mm

Agriculture   Pastoral extensive, commercial for sheep and a few cattle
◆ **Size**   170 hectares of enclosed land and grazing and rights over open mountainside. Flock of over 700 Swaledale sheep and 50 cattle
◆ **Machinery**   Tractor and machinery for silage (grass cut and stored) and hay (dried grass)
◆ **Labour**   Farmer with occasional help
◆ **Year**   March/April lambing; June/July shearing, dipping, silage and hay making; rest of year tending animals
◆ **Outputs**   Wool and mutton. Lambs and calves sold to lowland farms for fattening

B Dairy and beef farming, e.g. Devon

Area   The west of the UK

Relief   Low hills and gentle slopes

Soils   Heavy clay soils

Climate   Average temperatures: January 8°C, July 16°C. Annual rainfall over 750 mm

Agriculture   Commercial dairy farming
◆ **Size**   150 hectares. A herd of 110 milking cows is kept, milked twice a day. Cattle are fed on silage, hay, and concentrated high-protein food in winter. Some kale and root crops grown for winter feed when cows brought inside
◆ **Machinery**   Tractor, ploughs, and planting machinery, silage and hay-cutting equipment
◆ **Labour**   Family
◆ **Outputs**   Milk sold to local dairy and cheese factory

C Mixed farming, e.g. Northamptonshire

Area   Central England

Relief   Low hills, gentle slopes

Soils   Mixture of clay and chalky soils — medium loams

Climate   Average temperatures: January 5°C, July 17°C. Annual rainfall 750 mm

Agriculture   Commercial pastoral and arable
◆ **Size**   250 hectares. Grows wheat, barley, potatoes and kale and keeps a herd of 80 cattle which are reared and fattened for beef
◆ **Machinery**   Three tractors, range of machinery for arable farming, silage/hay-making equipment
◆ **Outputs**   Grain sold to local merchant, and cattle in the market. Kale fed to cattle

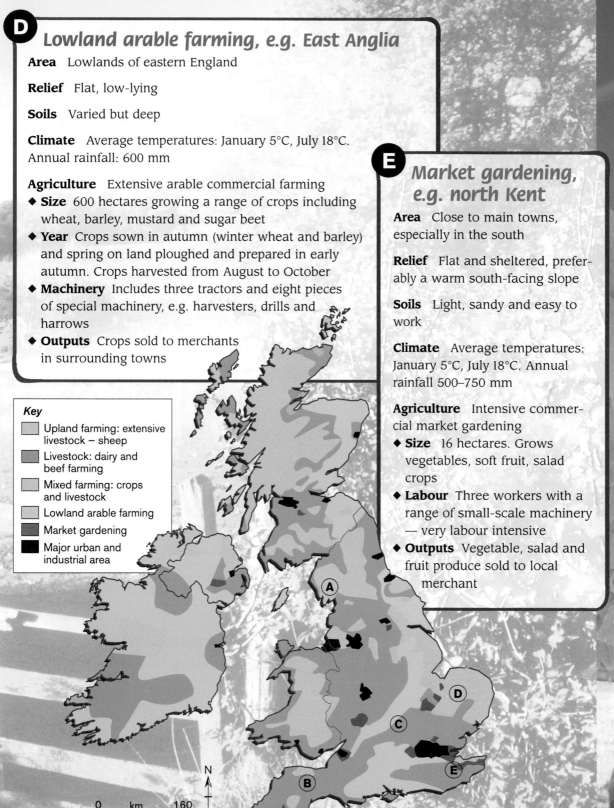

D Lowland arable farming, e.g. East Anglia

Area Lowlands of eastern England

Relief Flat, low-lying

Soils Varied but deep

Climate Average temperatures: January 5°C, July 18°C. Annual rainfall: 600 mm

Agriculture Extensive arable commercial farming
- **Size** 600 hectares growing a range of crops including wheat, barley, mustard and sugar beet
- **Year** Crops sown in autumn (winter wheat and barley) and spring on land ploughed and prepared in early autumn. Crops harvested from August to October
- **Machinery** Includes three tractors and eight pieces of special machinery, e.g. harvesters, drills and harrows
- **Outputs** Crops sold to merchants in surrounding towns

E Market gardening, e.g. north Kent

Area Close to main towns, especially in the south

Relief Flat and sheltered, preferably a warm south-facing slope

Soils Light, sandy and easy to work

Climate Average temperatures: January 5°C, July 18°C. Annual rainfall 500–750 mm

Agriculture Intensive commercial market gardening
- **Size** 16 hectares. Grows vegetables, soft fruit, salad crops
- **Labour** Three workers with a range of small-scale machinery — very labour intensive
- **Outputs** Vegetable, salad and fruit produce sold to local merchant

Key
- Upland farming: extensive livestock — sheep
- Livestock: dairy and beef farming
- Mixed farming: crops and livestock
- Lowland arable farming
- Market gardening
- Major urban and industrial area

N

0   km   160

Changes in agriculture and the countryside

There have been great changes in the methods used in farming over the last 50 years.

New types and varieties of crops are grown today and the number and quantity of pesticides and fertilisers has increased significantly since 1950. All have resulted in higher yields.

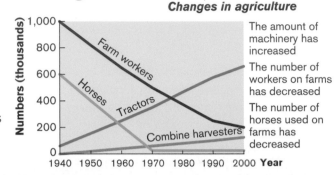

Changes in agriculture

The amount of machinery has increased

The number of workers on farms has decreased

The number of horses used on farms has decreased

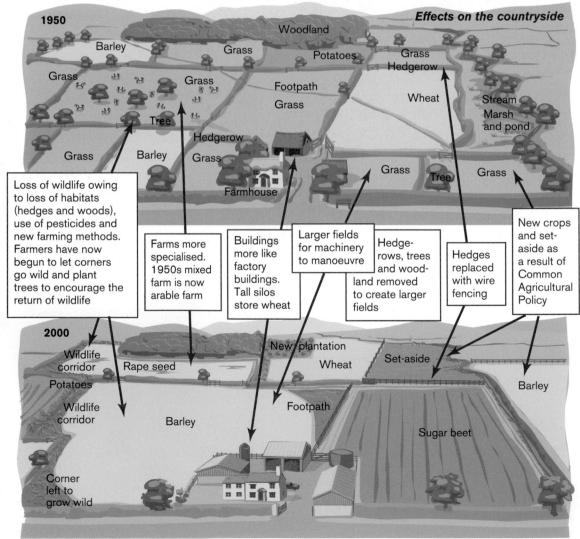

Effects on the countryside

1950

Woodland

Barley

Grass

Potatoes

Grass
Hedgerow

Grass

Grass

Footpath
Grass

Wheat

Stream
Marsh
and pond

Tree

Hedgerow
Grass

Grass

Tree

Grass

Grass

Barley

Farmhouse

Loss of wildlife owing to loss of habitats (hedges and woods), use of pesticides and new farming methods. Farmers have now begun to let corners go wild and plant trees to encourage the return of wildlife

Farms more specialised. 1950s mixed farm is now arable farm

Buildings more like factory buildings. Tall silos store wheat

Larger fields for machinery to manoeuvre

Hedge-rows, trees and wood-land removed to create larger fields

Hedges replaced with wire fencing

New crops and set-aside as a result of Common Agricultural Policy

2000

Wildlife corridor

New plantation

Set-aside

Potatoes

Rape seed

Wheat

Wildlife corridor

Barley

Footpath

Barley

Corner left to grow wild

Sugar beet

Farming in the European Union

The Common Agricultural Policy (CAP) governs farming in the countries of the European Union, including the UK.

Issue: Surpluses

The CAP protects farmers from competition from cheap foreign imports by guaranteeing a standard price for farm products. It resulted in farmers producing too much food, because they made more money the more they produced. This surplus was stored by the EU in warehouses as 'food mountains'

Solution 1: Quotas

In the 1980s farmers in the EU were producing too much milk. Milk quotas were introduced in 1984 to limit the production from each farm. Farmers can increase their quota by buying another farmer's quota

Solution 2: Set-aside

To limit the quantity of cereal crops (e.g. wheat, barley, oats) being produced, the EU pays farmers a subsidy to leave land uncultivated. All arable farmers must leave a proportion (15% of farms over 20 hectares) uncultivated as **set-aside.** They cannot farm this land but it can be used for other purposes, e.g. golf courses or camp sites which will earn the farmer money, wildlife areas for which the farmer will be given an extra subsidy, or left under grass for which the farmer is paid a grant

Solution 3: Environmentally sensitive areas

If a farm is in an environmentally sensitive area the farmer can obtain a **subsidy** for farming in an environmentally friendly way, e.g. reducing the use of pesticides. This will probably reduce the yield and benefit the environment

The Common Agricultural Policy of the European Union

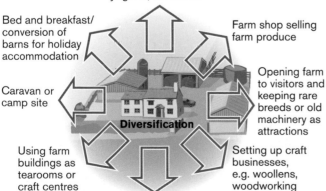

Making food products on the farm, e.g. cheese, yoghurt, ice cream

Bed and breakfast/ conversion of barns for holiday accommodation

Farm shop selling farm produce

Caravan or camp site

Opening farm to visitors and keeping rare breeds or old machinery as attractions

Diversification

Using farm buildings as tearooms or craft centres

Setting up craft businesses, e.g. woollens, woodworking

Pony trekking/horse riding

Diversification

Diversification is when farmers develop business activities other than farming on their land. They may do this to turn set-aside land to profitable use, or to increase their income.

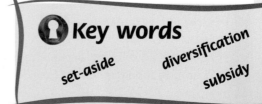

🔑 **Key words**

set-aside diversification subsidy

Farming in LEDCs

Subsistence farming

Most people in less economically developed countries (LEDCs) are farmers and most of these are subsistence farmers, e.g. 70% in India. **Subsistence farming** means producing crops and rearing animals for the use of the farmer. Only the surplus produce, if there is any, is sold.

There are three main types of subsistence farming:

Intensive arable farming The most common kind. Usually small patches of land near to the village are farmed. Most of the work is done by hand or using oxen, e.g. rice farming in southeast Asia.

Extensive shifting cultivation An area of land is cleared by cutting and burning the vegetation. Crops are planted and harvested. When the land loses its fertility after about 5 years the area is abandoned and another area is cleared and farmed, e.g. shifting cultivation in the Amazon rainforest, Brazil.

Extensive pastoral nomadism In regions where grazing is poor, farmers herd animals over wide areas in search of pasture, e.g. sheep herding in north Africa.

What all types of subsistence farming have in common

Low output
Farmer grows enough to feed the family, with little to sell

Very small surplus
Small sales at market

Little income
Little money to buy new seeds, machinery, fertilisers or pesticides

Low technology
Lack of money means use of traditional methods and little improvement in quality or yield

Plantation farming

Plantation farming involves **monoculture** — growing one type of crop over a large area, e.g. bananas, sugar cane, coffee.

It requires a lot of investment, usually from a wealthy company in an MEDC. Plantations are well organised to get the highest possible yields.

Plantations have advantages and disadvantages for LEDCs:

Advantages
✔ can provide employment
✔ provide investment in modern machinery and training of workers
✔ provide export earnings for LEDCs

Disadvantages
✘ can destroy large areas of natural vegetation
✘ much of the profit goes out of the country to the overseas company
✘ can lead to low pay and exploitation of workers
✘ if the price for the crop on the world market falls it can be disastrous
✘ monoculture plantations are vulnerable to pests, diseases or climate hazard, which can wipe out a whole year's crop

Increasing yields

The Green Revolution

1 In the mid-1960s scientists working in Mexico and the Philippines and backed by money from the USA developed new varieties of wheat, maize and rice

2 With these new varieties farmers could increase yields from each hectare by two or three times

3 These hybrid varieties became known as **HYVs** or 'high-yielding varieties'

4 In less than 5 years yields of rice, wheat and maize rose by up to 40% in many countries in Asia including India and Pakistan

5 Although there were many advantages of HYVs there were also disadvantages

Advantages of HYVs

✔ HYVs could increase yields by two or three times
✔ HYVs were not easily flattened by wind or rain because they had shorter, stronger stems
✔ HYVs grew more rapidly, e.g. 105–110 days for HYV rice compared with 140–160 days for traditional rice
✔ two or three crops instead of one or two a year could be grown on each hectare

Disadvantages of HYVs

✘ HYVs needed more regular water supplies which meant expensive irrigation schemes
✘ HYVs needed high inputs of fertilisers and pesticides which subsistence farmers could not afford
✘ HYVs needed new machinery which subsistence farmers could not afford
✘ mechanics were not available to repair the machinery
✘ subsistence farmers did not want to risk using the new varieties because failure meant disaster
✘ new machinery replaced manual labour leading to unemployment and rural–urban migration

Appropriate technology

In LEDCs where skilled mechanics and money are scarce it is often more appropriate to develop simple equipment which is easy to maintain and uses local or cheap materials.

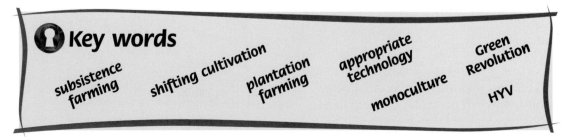

🔒 **Key words**

subsistence farming   shifting cultivation   plantation farming   appropriate technology   monoculture   Green Revolution   HYV

Agriculture and the environment

Soil erosion

Soil takes hundreds of years to form and is impossible to replace. Once soil is left bare it may be blown or washed away.

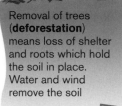

Removal of trees (**deforestation**) means loss of shelter and roots which hold the soil in place. Water and wind remove the soil

Overgrazing by animals means removal of the vegetation which binds the soil together. Water and wind remove the soil

Causes of soil erosion

Farming on steep slopes allows heavy rainfall to wash away soil and create deep gullies

Removal of hedges and overuse of fertilisers creates a light soil vulnerable to wind erosion

Leave shelter belts of trees as wind breaks

Reduce the number of animals to prevent overgrazing

Controlling soil erosion

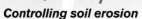

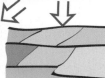

Build **terraces** on hillsides or plough across slopes creating ridges to stop water running downhill

Crop rotation – planting different crops at different times of year means the soil is never left bare

Leave stubble on **fallow** field to bind soil, and plant through the stubble

Irrigation

Irrigation means artificially watering the land with water taken from reservoirs, rivers or from underground.

In hot areas high evaporation of irrigation water can leave salty deposits in the soil and reduce yields. One badly-affected country is Pakistan.

Desertification

In areas where vegetation is sparse and rainfall uncertain, particularly on the edge of deserts, the balance between the amount of vegetation and number of grazing animals is delicate.

If the population increases and more trees are chopped down for fuelwood, or if more animals are kept in the wet years, the area cannot cope in dry years. Vegetation is killed by overgrazing, soil erosion occurs and the land becomes desert. Desertification is a particular problem in the Sahel on the edge of the Sahara Desert in Africa.

🔑 **Key words**

deforestation
irrigation
terraces
crop rotation
erosion
desertification
overgrazing
fallow

Test yourself

Choose the correct answer to these questions from the list below:

monoculture	shelter belts	terraces	mixed farming
pesticides	flowers	temperature	soil
decline in farm workers	need regular water supply	hill sheep farming	larger fields
ploughing	subsidies	diversification	labour
commercial	extensive	decrease in hedgerows	set-aside
shearing	precipitation	transport	fertilisers
high input of fertiliser	increase in tractors	wool	market gardening

1 List three human inputs, two capital inputs and three physical inputs of farms.

2 List three farm processes and two outputs of farms.

3 What type of farm produces animals and crops for sale?

4 What type of farm is very large and has a low yield per hectare?

5 What type of farming, growing vegetables and salad crops, is found close to cities?

6 What type of farming is found on the hills and mountains of western Scotland?

7 What land is left uncultivated by European Union regulation to limit output?

8 What name is given to the development of businesses other than agriculture on a farm?

9 List two changes on farms and two changes in the countryside in the last 50 years.

10 What is the name given to the growing of one type of crop over a large area?

11 Give two disadvantages of HYVs grown as part of the Green Revolution.

12 Name two methods of controlling soil erosion.

Examination question

(a) Three physical factors that affect farmers are climate, relief and soils.

    (i) **How does relief affect the type of farming in an area?** (3 marks)

    (ii) **How does climate affect the type of farming in an area?** (3 marks)

(b) Government policies can also influence farming. Describe one way in which European Union policies have influenced farming. (2 marks)

Foundation tier:

(c) It was said that the Green Revolution would change farming forever.

    (i) **What was the Green Revolution?** (2 marks)

    (ii) **Give three advantages brought by the Green Revolution.** (4 marks)

    (iii) What disadvantages did the Green Revolution have for farmers in LEDCs? (5 marks)

Higher tier:

(c) Describe and explain the advantages and disadvantages of the Green Revolution for farmers in LEDCs. (9 marks)

 Exam tip

You will notice that even the 'short' questions carry 2 marks. Make sure you include at least two main points in your answer to gain these marks. Always answer questions using complete sentences.

Types of industry

Industry can be divided into four main types:

Primary industry The gathering of the raw materials from which things are made. Raw materials occur naturally and can be:
- naturally occurring in the Earth, such as rocks which are quarried, oil which is drilled, or coal which is mined
- grown, such as farm crops or wood from forestry
- collected, for example fish from the sea, or rubber as latex from trees

Secondary industry Uses raw materials to make products, for example steel from iron ore. This may then be the raw material for another factory making cars.

Tertiary industry Does not make anything, but provides a service, such as retailing (shops), transport, teaching, hospitals, the police and civil servants.

Quaternary industry Very new research and development industries involved in biotechnology, information technology or communications.

Employment structure

The balance between the types of industry described above is shown by the percentage of people employed in them. This is known as the **employment structure**. These graphs show how it is changing in the UK. Fifty years ago the primary and secondary sectors of industry were large. Today the tertiary sector dominates.

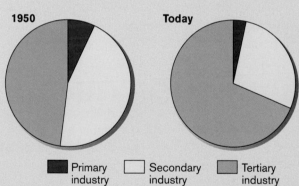

Change in employment structure in the UK

1950   Today

■ Primary industry   □ Secondary industry   ▨ Tertiary industry

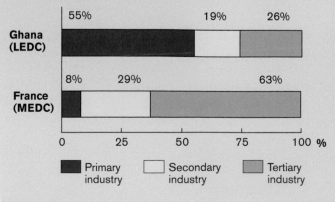

Employment structure in an LEDC and an MEDC

Ghana (LEDC): 55%   19%   26%

France (MEDC): 8%   29%   63%

0   25   50   75   100 %

■ Primary industry   □ Secondary industry   ▨ Tertiary industry

Employment structure is often used to show the level of development in a country. LEDCs have a large percentage of people in primary industry (generally farming). In MEDCs the largest percentage are employed in tertiary industry. As countries become more developed the percentage of primary industry falls and that of secondary and tertiary industry increases.

A *primary industry: quarrying*

Arguments for and against quarrying in an area of outstanding natural beauty:

For

✔ Provides jobs in a rural area where work is scarce.

✔ There is a national need for stone for roads and other building.

✔ Good stone and rock can only be quarried in hilly areas and these are usually attractive.

✔ When the quarry closes it must be landscaped to tone in with the local environment.

Against

✗ For the amount of disruption caused, few people work in the quarry.

✗ Creates an eyesore in the landscape visible for miles.

✗ Lorries carrying stone are large, noisy and damage the road surface.

✗ Dust from the crusher spoils the surrounding area.

✗ What is taken away cannot be replaced. Whole hillsides are disappearing.

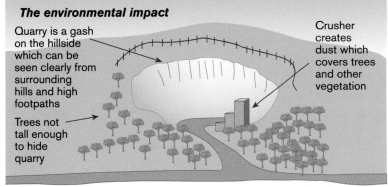

The quarry

Area to be landscaped when quarry closes

Well-maintained fencing and danger-warning signs

High back wall. Extraction within agreed limits

Buildings set within quarry not seen from road

High sides and narrow entrance to hide quarry from road

Trees to screen quarry from road

Lorries follow agreed routes to main road, avoiding villages

The environmental impact

Quarry is a gash on the hillside which can be seen clearly from surrounding hills and high footpaths

Crusher creates dust which covers trees and other vegetation

Trees not tall enough to hide quarry

Large, noisy, dirty lorries on narrow country lanes

Industry as a system

An industry has **inputs** (what is brought to the factory), **processes** and **outputs**.

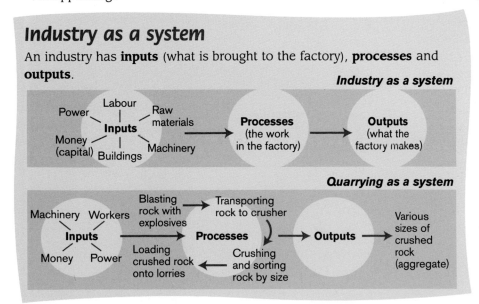

Industry as a system

Power Labour Raw materials

Inputs

Money (capital) Buildings Machinery

Processes (the work in the factory)

Outputs (what the factory makes)

Quarrying as a system

Machinery Workers

Inputs

Money Power

Blasting rock with explosives

Transporting rock to crusher

Loading crushed rock onto lorries

Processes

Crushing and sorting rock by size

Outputs

Various sizes of crushed rock (aggregate)

🔑 Key words

primary industry

secondary industry

tertiary industry

quaternary industry

employment structure

inputs processes

outputs

Secondary industry

Secondary industries range from traditional industries, such as the making of clothes from wool and cotton, to modern industries, such as car and electrical goods manufacturing.

Key factors for industrial location

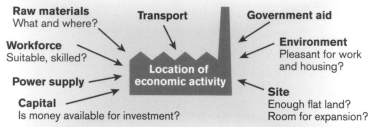

Raw materials What and where?

Transport

Government aid

Workforce Suitable, skilled?

Environment Pleasant for work and housing?

Power supply

Location of economic activity

Capital Is money available for investment?

Site Enough flat land? Room for expansion?

An example of location of traditional industry: cotton

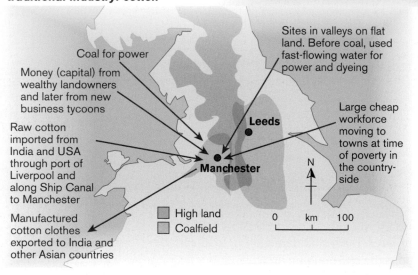

Coal for power

Money (capital) from wealthy landowners and later from new business tycoons

Raw cotton imported from India and USA through port of Liverpool and along Ship Canal to Manchester

Manufactured cotton clothes exported to India and other Asian countries

Sites in valleys on flat land. Before coal, used fast-flowing water for power and dyeing

Leeds

Large cheap workforce moving to towns at time of poverty in the country-side

Manchester

N

High land
Coalfield

0   km   100

Location

Traditional industry grew during the nine-teenth century. It depended on the supply of raw materials and coal for power. These were bulky and expensive to move, so the indus-tries located near to where they were found or could easily be imported.

An example of location of heavy industry: chemicals at Teesport

Today many of the UK's raw materials have either been used up, like iron ore, or are imported from overseas. Many **heavy industries** using bulky raw materials from abroad, for example the steel, oil and chemical industries, have devel-oped at the coast.

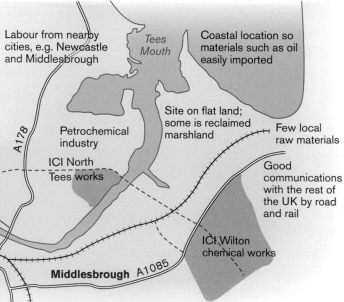

Labour from nearby cities, e.g. Newcastle and Middlesbrough

Tees Mouth

Coastal location so materials such as oil easily imported

A178

Petrochemical industry

ICI North Tees works

Site on flat land; some is reclaimed marshland

Few local raw materials

Good communications with the rest of the UK by road and rail

Railway

ICI Wilton chemical works

Middlesbrough A1085

Modern secondary industries are not tied to their source of raw materials or power and can locate where they like. Local and regional authorities may offer money and other incentives for a firm to locate in their area because they want the jobs and affluence the industry will bring.

 # Case Study: Toyota Cars at Burnaston

Good transport network to national and international markets

Area has skilled workforce, particularly in engineering

A38 to Derby

Site close to Coventry, Leicester, Nottingham, Birmingham, Derby, so many component suppliers and engineering services nearby

A50 to M6 and north

Greenfield site on flat land with room to expand

M1 and east

When industries which are linked are grouped together in one area it is called **agglomeration**

A **greenfield site** is one where no industry has been developed before

Support from local government:
- help with building roads, drains
- Derbyshire County Council bought £20 million stake in company
- support team to help Japanese workers and families settle into local community

Pleasant area to live, close to Peak District National Park, golf courses and sports facilities

A38 to Birmingham and motorways south and west

Industrial estates are areas in which industries are grouped, usually on the outskirts of urban areas. There is no residential or retail building

The opening of a new factory causes a boost to industry in the local area, e.g. more money spent in shops and new houses built, creating even more jobs. This is known as the **multiplier effect**

The motor car industry is a good example of **linkage**. What is made in one industry is used by another, and this links the industries together. For example, a component firm making car headlights or speedometers supplies the firm making cars. They depend on each other and difficulties in one will affect the other

Changes in south Derbyshire following the building of the Toyota factory

Environmental
◆ farmland lost
◆ number of vehicles in the area increased
◆ factory developed with low buildings
◆ pollution and waste controlled
◆ trees screen the factory

Social
◆ Toyota sponsors local education, cultural and leisure activities

Economic
◆ new engineering and car component firms move to the area
◆ electricity and water companies gain new contracts to supply the factory
◆ over 2,500 new jobs created in the area
◆ new houses built in the area — building jobs

 # Key words

traditional industry   agglomeration   heavy industry   industrial estate   greenfield site   linkage   multiplier effect

Tertiary industry

Shops are one type of service or tertiary industry. There are also many people working in tertiary industries in offices and public buildings like hospitals and schools.

A fast-growing service is call centres. With modern communications these can locate anywhere. The reasons for choosing a location are given in the case study below.

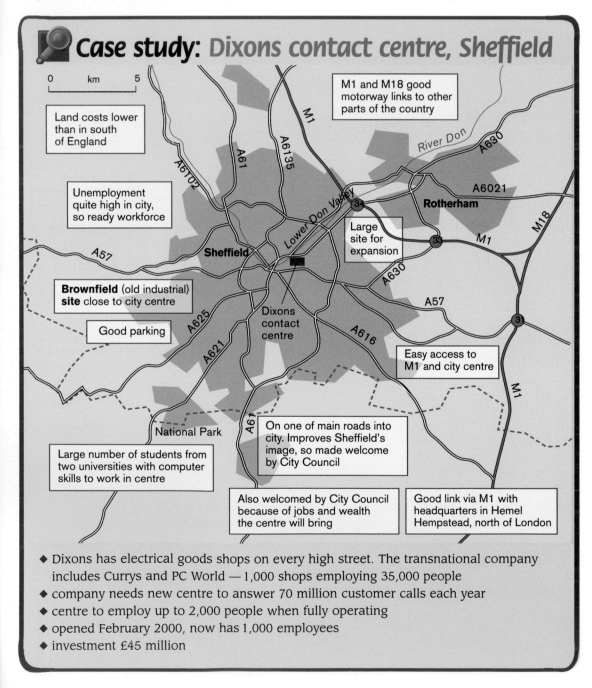

Case study: Dixons contact centre, Sheffield

M1 and M18 good motorway links to other parts of the country

Land costs lower than in south of England

Unemployment quite high in city, so ready workforce

Large site for expansion

Brownfield (old industrial) site close to city centre

Good parking

Dixons contact centre

Easy access to M1 and city centre

On one of main roads into city. Improves Sheffield's image, so made welcome by City Council

Large number of students from two universities with computer skills to work in centre

Also welcomed by City Council because of jobs and wealth the centre will bring

Good link via M1 with headquarters in Hemel Hempstead, north of London

Rotherham

Sheffield

National Park

River Don

Lower Don Valley

◆ Dixons has electrical goods shops on every high street. The transnational company includes Currys and PC World — 1,000 shops employing 35,000 people
◆ company needs new centre to answer 70 million customer calls each year
◆ centre to employ up to 2,000 people when fully operating
◆ opened February 2000, now has 1,000 employees
◆ investment £45 million

Hi-tech industries

Hi-tech (high-technology) industries are those linked to science and technology, e.g. making computers, mobile phones. Hi-tech industries are called **footloose** industries. They can locate anywhere because they do not depend on large quantities of raw materials or power.

'Silicon glen' central Scotland

Cambridge

M4 corridor

 Case study:
Cambridge Science Park

- ◆ Started in 1970 on a disused site owned by Trinity College north of Cambridge.
- ◆ Activity restricted to research and development of new ideas employing scientists and skilled technicians.
- ◆ Buildings at low level, often unusual designs, with attractive landscaped areas between.
- ◆ Seventy organisations based at the park.
- ◆ Over half of the employees have a degree.

Reasons for locating at Cambridge
- ◆ Prestige: worldwide reputation of university for excellence in science and technology.
- ◆ Links with the university departments and the latest ideas.
- ◆ Highly-skilled and qualified workforce.
- ◆ Attractive, well-landscaped site to create a good image and impress clients.
- ◆ Accessibility: motorway links for supplies and customers.

Unimportant factors
- ◆ Access to raw materials and power.
- ◆ Railway links.

Location of Cambridge Science Park

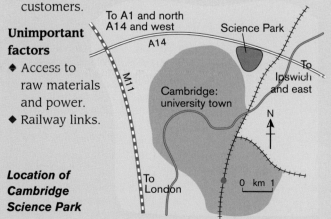

To A1 and north
A14 and west
A14
Science Park
To Ipswich and east
M11
Cambridge: university town
N
To London
0 km 1

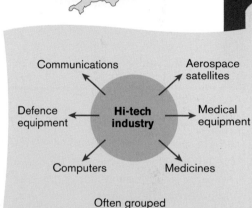

Communications

Aerospace satellites

Defence equipment

Hi-tech industry

Medical equipment

Computers

Medicines

Often grouped in science parks

Have a small workforce

Need only small quantities of raw materials

Location of hi-tech industries

Locate near good communications, especially by road

Need a highly-trained and skilled workforce

May locate near universities to share knowledge

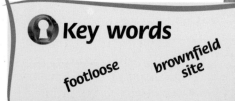 🔑 **Key words**

footloose

brownfield site

Changing location of industry in towns and cities

When urban areas were developing, industries grew up next to the streets where people lived. Few people had cars, and they walked the short distance to work. As towns expanded, large residential areas were built. There was no longer room for factories in the city centres and they relocated to the edges of the urban areas.

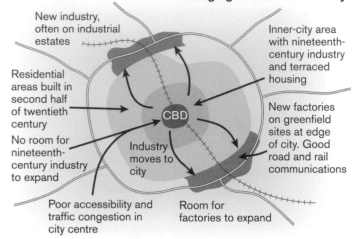

Changing location of industry

New industry, often on industrial estates

Residential areas built in second half of twentieth century

No room for nineteenth-century industry to expand

Inner-city area with nineteenth-century industry and terraced housing

New factories on greenfield sites at edge of city. Good road and rail communications

CBD

Industry moves to city

Poor accessibility and traffic congestion in city centre

Room for factories to expand

Case study: Lower Don Valley, Sheffield

Where industries in cities have declined and been cleared away, modern industries have grown up in their place, often with government assistance. Areas in which new building has taken place on old industrial sites are called **brownfield sites**.

New growth

In 1984 the City Council drew up plans to improve the environment of the valley

Decline

By 1920 the Lower Don Valley was full of steel and manufacturing industry and home to 40,000 people

By 1984 the City Council had moved almost all the residents from the polluted valley to new homes elsewhere

In 1870 Sheffield was supplying two thirds of Europe's steel

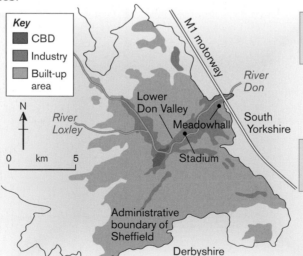

Key
- CBD
- Industry
- Built-up area

N

River Loxley

River Don

M1 motorway

Lower Don Valley

Meadowhall

South Yorkshire

Stadium

0 km 5

Administrative boundary of Sheffield

Derbyshire

In 1990 the Meadowhall shopping centre opened on the site of an old steelworks

In 1991 new sports facilities were built for the World Student Games

Supertram, a fast modern transport link, now runs the length of the valley

The valley is transformed: old factories renovated, new industry, and a new airport

The steel and engineering industries collapsed in the 1980s. 25,000 people lost their jobs and one third of the land in the valley was left vacant

£80 million of government funding through the Urban Development Corporation was used to build roads and attract new industry

Transnational companies

Transnational (or **multinational**) **companies**
◆ are very large, some with an income higher than that of small countries
◆ trade across the world with their headquarters in one country (usually an MEDC) and branch factories in many other countries, both MEDCs and LEDCs
◆ can benefit in several ways from owning factories in other countries: paying low wages, avoiding some taxes and tariffs, being near or inside a market

There are disadvantages as well as advantages for the host country.

Advantages
✔ provide jobs and good wages
✔ provide training to improve skills
✔ develop new roads and services and bring investment into the country
✔ increase foreign trade and bring foreign currency
✔ support other industries in the host country (the multiplier effect)

Disadvantages
✘ often locate research and development in home country but pay low wages for manufacturing in other countries
✘ bring foreign nationals to fill higher-paid jobs
✘ make goods for export, not for the host country
✘ take profits out of the host country
✘ close overseas factories first in difficult times

Case study: *Mars incorporated*

Snack foods Galaxy, Bounty, M&M's, Maltesers, Milky Way, Mars, Twix

Acumen business information and analysis service

Pet care Pedigree, Whiskas, Kitekat, Pal, Trill

Main meal Uncle Ben's, Dolmio, Yeomans

Vending systems in-cup drinks, e.g. tea, coffee

Plant-care Seramis

Mars Electronics International (electronic payment systems)

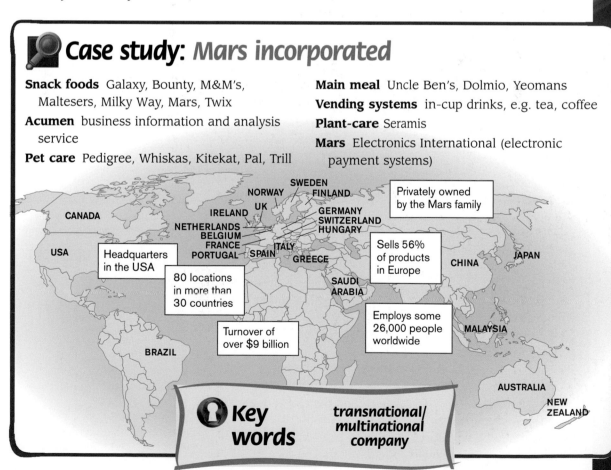

Privately owned by the Mars family

Headquarters in the USA

80 locations in more than 30 countries

Turnover of over $9 billion

Sells 56% of products in Europe

Employs some 26,000 people worldwide

Key words transnational/ multinational company

Industry in LEDCs

Industry in LEDCs may be **formal** or **informal**.

Formal sector
- ◆ regular waged employment (long hours and relatively low pay)
- ◆ in factories or offices
- ◆ working for an employer
- ◆ many employers are foreign multinational companies

Low profits → Low output → Lack of investment in modern machinery → Lack of investment in modern infrastructure: roads, power, railways

Informal sector (e.g. flower selling, shoe shining, bicycle repair, delivery services, small craft industries)
- ◆ irregular, insecure income
- ◆ in small workshops or on the streets
- ◆ self-employed and finding work wherever the opportunity arises
- ◆ no job security
- ◆ no money to invest in improvements, so job cannot develop

In many LEDCs the informal sector employs more people than the formal sector. LEDCs find it hard to break out of the cycle of low profits and lack of investment.

Newly industrialised countries (NICs)

The growth of industry in Taiwan

1950	Few natural resources. Prosperous farming	Developing and expanding textiles and clothing manufacture	New industries based on cheap labour and raw materials	New heavy industries: shipbuilding, steel-making,	Better-educated workforce develops new skills. Quality improved, prices kept low	2000
Agriculture 24% Industry 30% Services 46%	①	②	③	④	⑤	Agriculture 4% Industry 42% Services 54%
	Processing rice and sugar cane	Cheap, low-tech production process using craft skills people already have	Plastics as by-product of oil Electrical goods from components made in Japan and USA	oil-refining, chemicals	Electrical goods, televisions New infrastructure including motorways	

Examples of NICs are the southeast Asian countries of South Korea, Taiwan, Singapore and Hong Kong. These so-called 'tiger economies' have broken out of the cycle of low profits and lack of investment. They have succeeded in this through:
- ◆ investment from other countries, mainly Japan and USA, because of the motivated workforce working for low wages
- ◆ investment in infrastructure (road, rail and ports) for communications
- ◆ early industries such as clothing, shoes, and paper products which relied on relatively cheap raw materials, abundance of cheap labour, low technology, and the use of craft skills already possessed by the workforce
- ◆ over time the workforce developed new skills to make electrical goods, televisions, computers and cars

🔑 Key words

formal sector

informal sector

newly industrialised country (NIC)

Test yourself

1 Give two examples of each of the following: primary industry, secondary industry, tertiary industry and quaternary industry.
2 How does the employment structure in most LEDCs differ from that in MEDCs?
3 Give two reasons why people would be in favour of quarrying in an area.
4 List four inputs of quarrying as a system.
5 Draw a star diagram to show as many reasons for industrial location as you can.
6 How has the location of industry in towns changed in the last 100 years?
7 What is a 'footloose' industry?
8 What is a 'transnational company'?
9 Give four advantages of a transnational company locating in a country.
10 What are the differences between the 'formal sector' and the 'informal sector' of industry in an LEDC?

Examination question

(a) **Four types of industry are primary, secondary, tertiary and quaternary.**
  Write the correct type alongside each statement below:
  (i) Working in offices and shops serving the public.
  (ii) Growing and cutting trees for making furniture.
  (iii) Carrying out research into new medicines.
  (iv) Making electrical goods for use in the home.   (2 marks)

(b) **Look at the graph which shows the types of industry in Peru, an LEDC.**
  (i) How does the graph of types of industry in Peru differ from that of an MEDC?   (2 marks)
  (ii) Give three advantages of attracting transnational companies to open branch factories in an LEDC.   (3 marks)

Types of industry in Peru

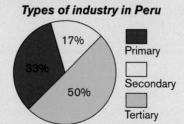

Primary
Secondary
Tertiary

 Exam tip

In the higher question, notice that you need to name an actual example. There are two parts in the last sentence: 'explain why...' and 'what benefits...'. If you miss one, you will lose marks.

Foundation tier:
(c) **Look at the diagram on p. 93 which shows the location of the Cambridge Science Park.**
  (i) Suggest the advantages the Science Park brings to Cambridge.   (5 marks)
  (ii) Suggest reasons why the Science Park was located on the outskirts of Cambridge.   (5 marks)

Higher tier:
(c) **For a newly-built factory you have studied:**
  (i) Name the factory or site.
  (ii) Describe and explain why the factory opened at that location, and what benefits it brought to the area.   (10 marks)

Resources and energy

All industries need **resources** in order to operate. Most resources come originally from the Earth, for example iron ore, copper, coal, oil and lead. A farmer will consider the land itself as a resource, and for a modern industry the skill of its workers is its most important resource.

Natural resources

Natural resources are those which occur in the environment, for example coal, oil, timber, water and even energy from the sun. They can be divided into two groups:

Renewable resources which do not run out, for example wind, water, plants (timber from trees) and energy from the sun.

Non-renewable resources which are finite — they cannot be replaced once they have been used and will eventually run out. Examples are oil, coal, copper and diamonds.

Natural resources provide us with the energy we use to power our industrial society.

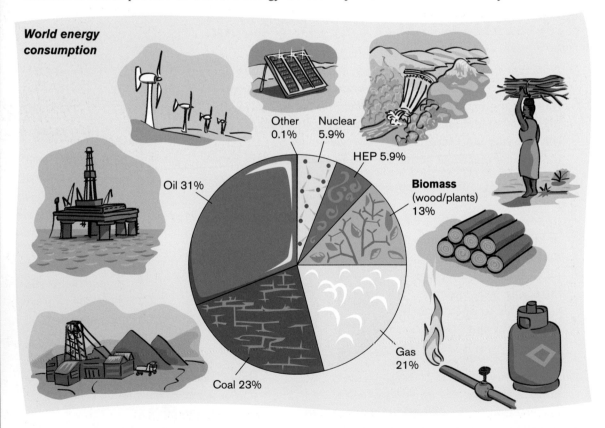

World energy consumption

Other 0.1%
Nuclear 5.9%
HEP 5.9%
Biomass (wood/plants) 13%
Oil 31%
Gas 21%
Coal 23%

MEDCs have 25% of the world's population and consume 80% of the world's energy supplies.

Many LEDCs rely on wood as a fuel, particularly for heating and cooking. The increase in population means that in some areas trees are being cut down faster than they are being replaced, leading to deforestation.

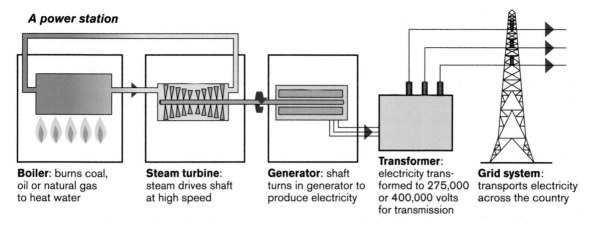

A power station

Boiler: burns coal, oil or natural gas to heat water

Steam turbine: steam drives shaft at high speed

Generator: shaft turns in generator to produce electricity

Transformer: electricity transformed to 275,000 or 400,000 volts for transmission

Grid system: transports electricity across the country

This type of power station uses non-renewable resources to produce electricity. Such resources are often called **fossil fuels** because they have formed over millions of years from vegetation (e.g. coal) or small animals (e.g. oil).

Changes

The type of fuel used for electricity generation in Britain is changing rapidly

- the amount of gas used has risen dramatically
- the amount of nuclear power used has increased
- the amount of coal used has declined dramatically
- the amount of oil used has decreased

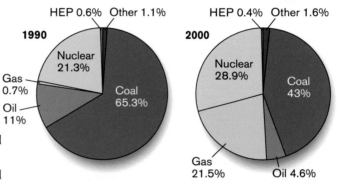

Electricity generation, 1990 and 2000

1990
HEP 0.6% Other 1.1%
Nuclear 21.3%
Gas 0.7%
Oil 11%
Coal 65.3%

2000
HEP 0.4% Other 1.6%
Nuclear 28.9%
Coal 43%
Gas 21.5%
Oil 4.6%

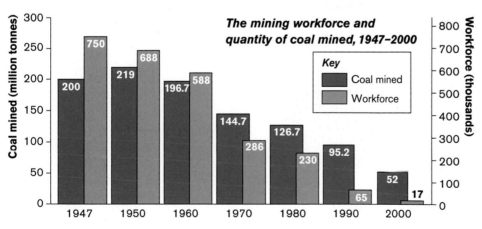

The mining workforce and quantity of coal mined, 1947–2000

Key
Coal mined
Workforce

Coal mined (million tonnes) / Workforce (thousands)

1947: 200 / 750
1950: 219 / 688
1960: 196.7 / 588
1970: 144.7 / 286
1980: 126.7 / 230
1990: 95.2 / 65
2000: 52 / 17

The decline in the use of coal and the use of imported coal have meant great changes to the coal-mining industry in the UK:

- the number of miners declined from 688,000 in 1950 to 17,000 in 2000
- the amount of coal mined fell from 219 million tonnes in 1950 to 52 million tonnes in 2000
- in the past 50 years about 1,000 coal mines in the UK have closed

🔑 Key words

renewable

non-renewable

natural resources

biomass

fossil fuels

GCSE Geography

Non-renewable energy resources

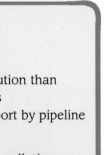

Oil

Advantages
- ✔ burns efficiently
- ✔ is relatively cheap to transport by pipeline, lorry and tanker ship
- ✔ has a variety of energy uses, e.g. in power stations, engines and cars

Disadvantages
- ✗ produces pollutant gases when it burns
- ✗ releases carbon dioxide which contributes to global warming
- ✗ spillage can cause widespread environmental damage and is difficult to clear up

Comments
- ◆ found in relatively few high-producing areas
- ◆ used also for plastics, paints, fertiliser and many other products

Coal

Advantages
- ✔ widely available
- ✔ there are large reserves worldwide

Disadvantages
- ✗ produces large quantities of pollutant gas and releases carbon dioxide
- ✗ underground mining is dangerous and makes coal expensive to use
- ✗ modern opencast mines cause environmental damage

Comments
- ◆ an early form of energy resource, today mainly used to generate electricity
- ◆ decreasing in importance

Fuelwood

Advantages
- ✔ widely available
- ✔ can be replanted and can be sustainable
- ✔ in LEDCs is often free and can be collected daily from the local area

Disadvantages
- ✗ increasing use can lead to deforestation and soil erosion
- ✗ releases carbon dioxide

Comment
- ◆ often used in LEDCs as a free source of cooking fuel but is time-consuming to collect

Natural gas

Advantages
- ✔ burns efficiently
- ✔ causes less pollution than other fossil fuels
- ✔ is easy to transport by pipeline

Disadvantages
- ✗ causes some air pollution
- ✗ releases carbon dioxide
- ✗ is highly flammable and can cause explosions

Comment
- ◆ used increasingly in the UK as an energy source in gas-fired power stations and domestic heating

Nuclear power

Advantages
✔ is 'clean' and efficient
✔ no bulky waste products

Disadvantages
✘ dangerous if radiation leaks occur (e.g. Chernobyl)
✘ very expensive to build and to close down, to make old stations safe and to dispose of the waste

Comments
◆ increasing use during the second half of the twentieth century but public fears and high costs have restricted growth, e.g. in the UK
◆ major energy source in some countries, e.g. France

Non-renewable energy resources
◆ Over three-quarters of the world's power is produced from coal, oil and gas. Supplies of these fossil fuels will eventually run out, but we will probably have to stop using them long before that because of the pollution they cause.
◆ The burning of fossil fuels releases pollutant gases including carbon dioxide, which contributes to global warming, and sulphur dioxide, which causes acid rain.
◆ Nuclear power, which uses uranium (a radioactive material found in certain rocks), was once seen as an alternative to fossil fuels. The dangers of radiation have made it much less popular.

Case study: Oil from Alaska

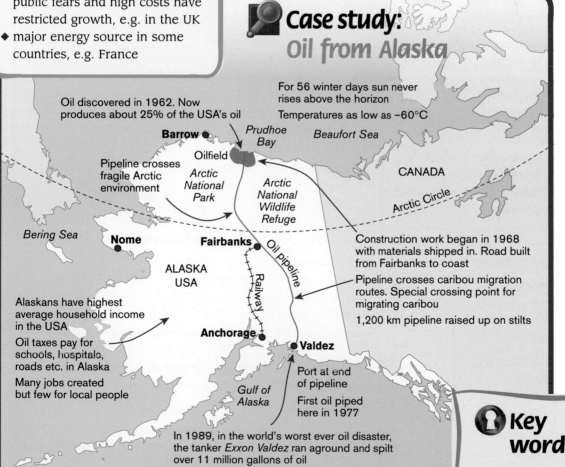

Oil discovered in 1962. Now produces about 25% of the USA's oil

For 56 winter days sun never rises above the horizon
Temperatures as low as −60°C

Barrow
Prudhoe Bay
Beaufort Sea

Oilfield

Pipeline crosses fragile Arctic environment

Arctic National Park

Arctic National Wildlife Refuge

CANADA

Arctic Circle

Bering Sea

Nome

Fairbanks
Oil pipeline

ALASKA USA

Railway

Construction work began in 1968 with materials shipped in. Road built from Fairbanks to coast

Pipeline crosses caribou migration routes. Special crossing point for migrating caribou

1,200 km pipeline raised up on stilts

Alaskans have highest average household income in the USA

Oil taxes pay for schools, hospitals, roads etc. in Alaska

Many jobs created but few for local people

Anchorage

Valdez

Gulf of Alaska

Port at end of pipeline

First oil piped here in 1977

In 1989, in the world's worst ever oil disaster, the tanker *Exxon Valdez* ran aground and spilt over 11 million gallons of oil

Around 3,000 km of coastline contaminated. Wildlife, including 10 million birds, devastated

Clean-up cost over $1 billion. Compensation around $1 billion

0   km   600

Key word

fuelwood

Renewable energy resources

Hydroelectric power

Advantages

✔ water is widely available in remote upland areas
✔ very clean
✔ provides cheap power
✔ reservoirs can be multi-purpose, e.g. for power, recreation and water supply

Disadvantages

✘ reservoirs flood valleys — loss of land and villages
✘ areas flooded may be scenic — loss of amenity and habitats
✘ silt building up behind the dam causes problems

Comment

◆ uses fast-flowing water to turn turbines — expensive to build but easy to run and provides cheap electricity

Wind power

Advantages

✔ very clean, no air pollution
✔ cheap to run and generally quiet

Disadvantages

✘ some people think turbines are visually polluting
✘ wind is not constant and may drop
✘ huge areas of turbines needed to produce much power

Comments

◆ widespread use in only a few areas, e.g. Denmark and California
◆ improving with more advanced technology

Solar power (from the sun)

Advantages

✔ cheap to run, clean and efficient
✔ no noise or air pollution

Disadvantages

✘ less useful in cloudy countries
✘ costly to install — high-tech

Comments

◆ can be used on a small scale in individual homes or to power factories — not yet feasible for large-scale production of power

Tidal power

Advantages

✔ clean and cheap to run
✔ can produce large quantities of electricity

Disadvantages

✘ expensive to build
✘ very few sites are suitable
✘ affects wildlife habitats in the estuary

Comment

◆ needs a high tidal range in a narrow estuary — much discussion about using the Severn Estuary

Geothermal power (from water heated underground by volcanic action)

Advantage

✔ clean and efficient with a constant supply of hot water

Disadvantages

✘ some polluting gas as a by-product
✘ only available in geothermally active areas

Comment

◆ many sites around the world, particularly in Iceland, New Zealand and Japan

Renewable energy sources

◆ Only account for a small part of the electrical energy produced worldwide.
◆ Are cleaner than non-renewable energy sources.
◆ Are environmentally friendly, particularly in relation to air pollution.
◆ Are expensive to develop but cheap to run.
◆ Are **sustainable** — they will not run out.
◆ Have potential for the future as technology develops.

 ## Case study: The Narmada Project, India

Advantages

✔ large quantities of electricity generated
✔ large areas of farmland irrigated
✔ flooding by river controlled
✔ fishing in the lakes created by the dams
✔ water for domestic and industrial use
✔ 36,000 hectares of new forest planted to replace what is lost

Disadvantages

✘ local people oppose the scheme
✘ over 1 million people will have to leave their homes as their villages are submerged
✘ the land offered to displaced people is poor
✘ environmental damage to 24,000 hectares of forest — the replanting cannot replace lost habitats
✘ benefits will be slight, e.g. 123,000 hectares of land irrigated but 90,000 submerged
✘ dams may silt up quickly, reducing storage capacity of reservoirs
✘ the region is an earthquake zone

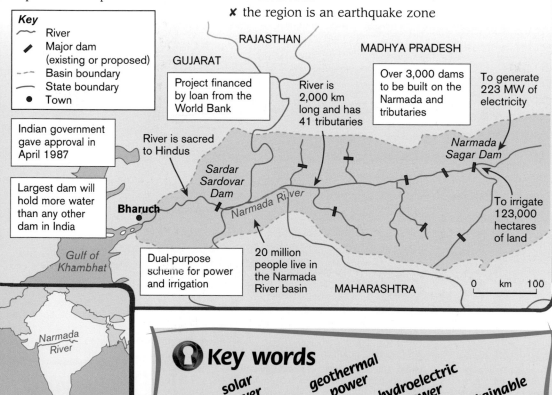

Key
~ River
⟋ Major dam (existing or proposed)
--- Basin boundary
— State boundary
● Town

RAJASTHAN
MADHYA PRADESH
GUJARAT

Project financed by loan from the World Bank

River is 2,000 km long and has 41 tributaries

Over 3,000 dams to be built on the Narmada and tributaries

To generate 223 MW of electricity

Indian government gave approval in April 1987

River is sacred to Hindus

Narmada Sagar Dam

Largest dam will hold more water than any other dam in India

Sardar Sardovar Dam

Bharuch

Narmada River

To irrigate 123,000 hectares of land

Gulf of Khambhat

Dual-purpose scheme for power and irrigation

20 million people live in the Narmada River basin

MAHARASHTRA

0   km   100

Narmada River

Key words

solar power
geothermal power
hydroelectric power
sustainable

Acid rain

Acidic gases including sulphur dioxide and oxides of nitrogen are released by the burning of fossil fuels in power stations and vehicles. These gases may dissolve in water droplets in the atmosphere which later fall as acid rain.

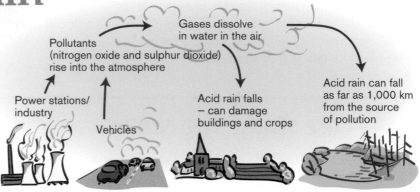

The causes of acid rain

Pollutants (nitrogen oxide and sulphur dioxide) rise into the atmosphere

Gases dissolve in water in the air

Power stations/industry

Vehicles

Acid rain falls – can damage buildings and crops

Acid rain can fall as far as 1,000 km from the source of pollution

An international issue

All countries in Europe are concerned about acid rain. A country may pollute its own atmosphere but the pattern of westerly winds means that the acid rain created in one country falls in another. For example, pollution from the UK affects forests and lakes in Sweden.

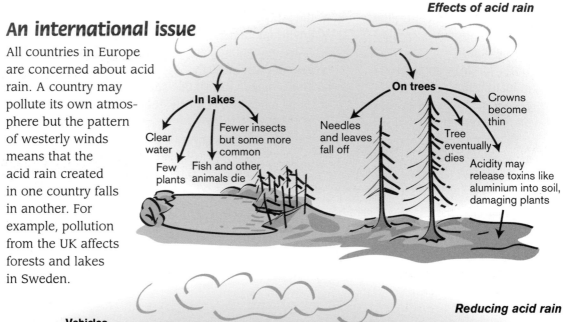

Effects of acid rain

In lakes

Clear water

Few plants

Fewer insects but some more common

Fish and other animals die

On trees

Needles and leaves fall off

Crowns become thin

Tree eventually dies

Acidity may release toxins like aluminium into soil, damaging plants

Reducing acid rain

Vehicles

Catalytic converter reduces emissions of harmful gases

Reduce speed

Fuel mixture electronically controlled to reduce pollution

Recirculate exhaust gases through engine to reduce nitrogen oxide emission

Fuel injection supplies exact amounts of fuel to engine to increase efficiency

Industry/power stations

Burn cleaner fuel, e.g. North Sea gas instead of coal

Purify flue gases so less pollution escapes

Treat fuel before it is burnt to reduce pollutants

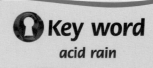

🔑 **Key word**
acid rain

Test yourself

1 What is the difference between renewable and non-renewable resources?

2 Give two changes which have taken place in the last 10 years in the use of energy resources in the UK.

3 Complete these diagrams:

Gas
Advantage: ....
....
Disadvantage: ....
....

Coal
Advantage: Is widely available

Disadvantage: Produces
much pollution

← **Non-renewable resources** →

Oil
Advantage: ....
....
Disadvantage: ....
....

Hydroelectric power
Advantage: Water widely
 available
Disadvantage: ....
....

Tidal power
Advantage: ....
....
Disadvantage: ....
....

← **Renewable resources** →

Solar power
Advantage: ....
....
Disadvantage: ....
....

4 Give two effects of acid rain, and two ways in which acid rain can be reduced.

Examination question

(a) Look at the graph.
 (i) Describe the changes shown by the graph. (2 marks)
 (ii) Explain why the changes have taken place. (3 marks)

Graph to show the number of miners and the amount of coal mined between 1950 and 2000

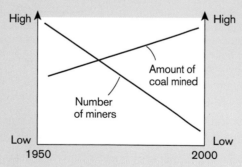

Exam tip

Look at the number of marks for each section and make sure you include at least one good point for each mark. Notice in the last section how important your knowledge of a case study is.

Foundation tier:
(b) For one major non-renewable resource project you have studied:
 (i) Give the name of the resource project and its location. (1 mark)
 (ii) Describe the main features of the project. (2 marks)
 (iii) Describe the advantages and disadvantages of the project. (6 marks)

Higher tier:
(b) For one major non-renewable resource project you have studied, name the project and describe its main features. Explain the main advantages and disadvantages of the project. (9 marks)

Measuring development

Measuring development must take into account many factors apart from wealth. Development depends also on factors such as education and health care. We would not say that a country was developed unless people living there were able to enjoy a reasonable quality of life.

> High birth rates are often a characteristic of LEDCs, but the USA has a surprisingly high rate too

> Egypt is not a wealthy country but it has a low number of people per doctor, only slightly more than the UK

> Nigeria, Egypt and Peru are **LEDCs**

Country	GNP (US$)	Birth rate (per 1,000)	Life expectancy (years)	Urban population (%)	Adult literacy (%)	People per doctor
Nigeria	260	45	52	41	52	5,997
Egypt	790	29	65	45	49	725
Peru	2,310	27	68	71	87	989
Argentina	8,030	20	73	88	95	337
South Korea	9,700	16	72	82	97	1,076
UK	18,700	13	77	89	99	623
Japan	39,640	10	80	78	99	613
USA	26,980	16	76	76	99	408

> Peru is generally thought of as an LEDC, but 71% of people live in towns, much higher than the level in many LEDCs

> UK, USA and Japan are **MEDCs**

> GNP measures wealth. It is measured in US$ per head so that countries can be compared. There are big differences between these six countries

> South Korea and Argentina have some characteristics of LEDCs, such as high birth rates, and some characteristics of MEDCs, such as high levels of adult literacy. They also have moderate wealth (GNP). They are examples of newly industrialising countries (**NICs**)

The table shows six **indicators of development** which can be used to try to decide how developed a country is. Other indicators, such as infant mortality rates or access to safe water, can also be used.

Study the table carefully and try to think about what these indicators tell you about a country. For example, why are literacy rates so low in some countries and how might this affect the country's development?

◆ Why are birth rates in MEDCs generally much lower than in LEDCs?

◆ How could life expectancy in LEDCs be increased?

🔑 **Key words**

literacy

indicators of development

life expectancy

LEDCs

MEDCs

NICs

The north–south divide

Some countries are wealthier than others. Rich countries, such as the UK and the USA, are known as **more economically developed countries** (MEDCs). Poorer countries are known as **less economically developed countries** (LEDCs).

The world map below shows the north–south line, which is often used as a rough guide to levels of development. In general those countries 'north' of the line are MEDCs and those 'south' of the line are LEDCs.

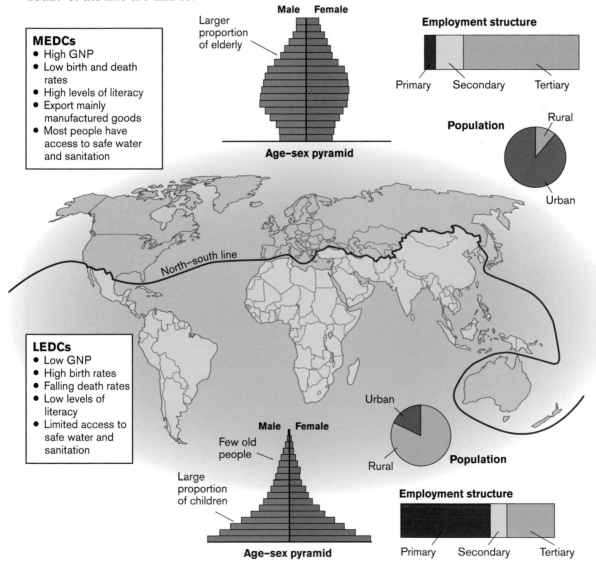

MEDCs
- High GNP
- Low birth and death rates
- High levels of literacy
- Export mainly manufactured goods
- Most people have access to safe water and sanitation

LEDCs
- Low GNP
- High birth rates
- Falling death rates
- Low levels of literacy
- Limited access to safe water and sanitation

One of the problems with this map is that it suggests that countries are either economically developed or they are not. In reality there is a huge range in levels of development and no two countries are the same.

Aid

Aid is the transfer of resources such as money, equipment, food, training or skilled people from MEDCs to LEDCs. Aid is given to help LEDCs either in an emergency or for long-term economic development.

Different types of aid are given in different ways.

Bilateral aid Aid given directly from one government to another in the form of money, training, technology, food or other supplies. In some cases this aid is **tied aid**, which means it has conditions attached which will usually benefit the donor country.

Multilateral aid Aid which comes from a number of different governments or organisations. It is usually arranged by an international organisation such as the World Bank or the United Nations (UN). These organisations usually give to large-scale projects.

Non-governmental aid Organisations such as Oxfam and Save the Children run projects all over the world, many of which are small-scale. They also help to organise **emergency aid** after disasters. These **non-governmental organisations (NGOs)** raise their money through donations and from government grants.

Case study:
The Three Gorges Dam, China

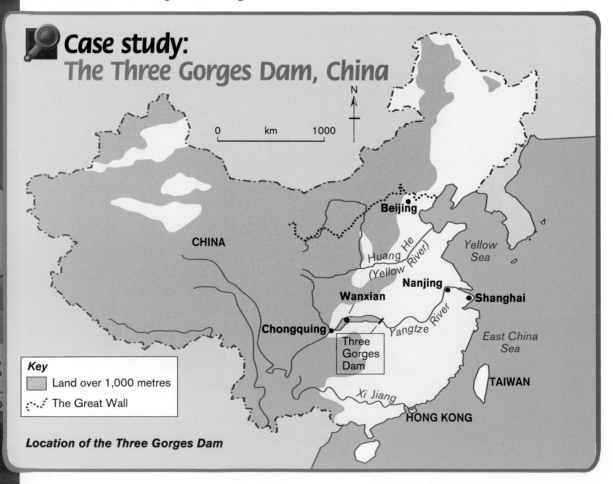

Location of the Three Gorges Dam

Every year the Yangtze River floods, causing huge problems. The dam will control flooding and protect over 10 million people who live near the river

HEP is a renewable and clean form of energy production. It will mean China can burn fewer fossil fuels so it will help to reduce atmospheric pollution and emissions of greenhouse gases

The area is very beautiful, but when the spectacular gorges are flooded, fewer tourists may visit. Tourism is a valuable source of foreign earnings for China

The dam will flood some precious archaeological sites

The new dam will provide electricity for many towns in China including Shanghai and Chongquing. This will help economic development

Wildlife will also be threatened, including the Chinese alligator, the Yangtze river dolphin and Chinese paddlefish

There are many different points of view about how this project will affect people and the environment

Over 1 million people will have to move away because their towns and villages will be flooded by the new lake. They will be moved on to higher land which is colder and less fertile than their land by the river

In 1992 the Chinese government agreed to build a huge dam on the Yangtze River. Work began in 1994 and is estimated to be finished in 2009. The new dam will create a lake 600 km long and over 1 km wide. The estimated cost is between US$20 billion and US$40 billion. When completed it will be the largest hydroelectric project in the world.

The dam is located in an earthquake zone. It's designed to be protected against earthquakes but it will hold so much water that the weight could trigger an earthquake that would damage the dam

China has had difficulty financing this massive project. Money has been obtained from businesses in Japan, Canada, Germany and Switzerland which hope to benefit from close links with China in the future. With a population of over 1.2 billion, China is a huge potential market. Individual arrangements like this between governments are examples of bilateral aid.

The dam will trap silt which will gradually fill up the reservoir. Areas downstream will be deprived of the naturally fertile silt and farmers will have to buy artificial fertilisers instead

Large projects such as this in LEDCs are often funded through the World Bank (multilateral aid), but the World Bank has decided not to fund the Three Gorges project. Other World Bank projects in China, which have also involved the resettlement of thousands of people, have created a lot of bad publicity, and the organisation does not want any more of this. Its decision not to put any money into this project can therefore be seen as political.

🔑 Key words

tied aid

bilateral aid

multilateral aid

non-governmental organisation (NGO)

emergency aid

development

World trade

The pattern of world **trade** is very uneven. MEDCs account for by far the largest amount of trade. They produce about 70% of the world's **exports**, which they sell mainly to other MEDCs but also to LEDCs. The newly industrialising countries (NICs) such as South Korea and Taiwan are also important trading nations. MEDCs and NICs mostly export manufactured goods which have a higher value than raw materials.

LEDCs have a much smaller share of world trade, only about 20%. They tend to sell raw materials or **primary products** and to **import** manufactured goods. Primary products have less value than manufactured goods and the price is controlled by MEDC buyers. If there are several LEDC producers of a product like bananas or sugar then prices come down, especially if a surplus is produced. The price of primary products often fluctuates, which can cause great difficulties for the producers, especially if they are dependent on one or two products only.

Trading blocs

Groups of countries often join together and make trade agreements to help each other. The countries of the European Union (EU), for example, have an agreement which allows free trade between member states.

Trade barriers

Governments may use tariffs (tax duties) to stop too many imports into their country. Quotas may also be used. These limit the amount of a product that may be imported. Governments use trade barriers to try to protect their own industries.

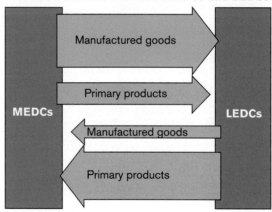

The trade balance between MEDCs and LEDCs

MEDCs — Manufactured goods → LEDCs
Primary products →
← Manufactured goods
← Primary products

The width of the arrow represents the volume of trade

Third World debt

In the 1960s and 1970s many LEDCs were persuaded to borrow money from MEDCs such as the USA, the UK and other European countries. At that time interest rates were low and the repayment terms seemed reasonable. During the last 30 years the repayment of debts has become increasingly difficult for many countries. They may now owe much more money than they first borrowed, because of the interest they have been charged. Debts are stopping poor countries such as Tanzania from developing. The government has to spend so much money repaying the country's debts that little is left for education and health services.

There have been demonstrations and campaigns in Europe and North America to bring the debt problem to public attention. Some governments, including the UK government, are now promising to cancel all 'Third World debt'.

Key words

trade
primary products
trade barrier
trading bloc
imports
exports

Test yourself

1 Match these terms to the correct definition:

bilateral aid   short-term immediate relief after a disaster

tied aid   aid given with conditions, usually to benefit the donor

NGO aid   aid given by one government to another

emergency aid   development projects run by charities such as Oxfam

multilateral aid   aid arranged by international organisations, e.g. the World Bank

2 What do you understand by these terms: life expectancy, primary products, aid, NGO?

3 Explain why world trade patterns tend to work in favour of MEDCs and against LEDCs.

Examination question

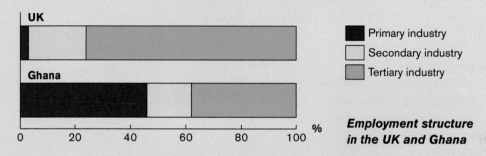

Employment structure in the UK and Ghana

(a) Compare the employment structure of the UK with that of Ghana. (3 marks)

(b) Give reasons to suggest why there are differences between employment structures in the two countries. (6 marks)

Foundation tier:

(c) (i) Name and locate a development project you have studied.
(ii) Outline how the project was paid for, including the type of aid given.
(iii) Describe the impacts the project has had on people and on the environment.

(8 marks)

Higher tier:

(c) Using a named example of a development project which you have studied, describe how the project has been funded and evaluate the success of the project. (8 marks)

 Exam tip

*Make sure you understand command words such as **compare**, **suggest why**, **describe** and **evaluate**.*

Growth of tourism

Tourism is a very important industry. It is estimated that about 600 million people make international visits every year and this number is growing. About 10% of the world's workforce is employed in the tourist industry, which generates a vast amount of money.

The graph shows how the numbers of international tourists have increased during the last 50 years and are expected to go on rising. There are several reasons for this:

◆ **Transport**, especially road networks and air travel, developed rapidly in the twentieth century, so travel is now quicker and easier.

◆ People in MEDCs are earning more and have **more money to spend** on themselves after they have paid their living costs, so they take more holidays.

◆ Many people, especially in MEDCs, have **more days of paid leave** so they can take longer holidays and travel further.

◆ Travel companies provide a huge range of **package holidays** and other organised trips, making travel much easier.

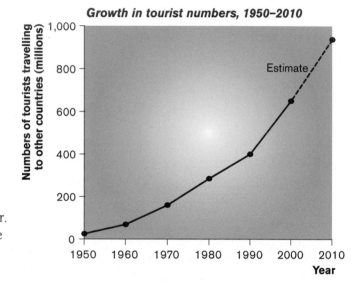

Growth in tourist numbers, 1950–2010

◆ People **know much more** about different places in the world through education, television programmes and the internet, and this encourages them to travel.

Ecotourism

Ecotourism is seen as an alternative way for LEDCs to develop tourism in a **sustainable** way. It is environmentally-friendly, low-impact and low-density tourism which aims to:

◆ protect natural environments including animals and plants
◆ help local people earn money directly and indirectly
◆ put money into the community to improve facilities such as sanitation, transport and health care
◆ allow local people to make decisions about how the area is developed

Ecotourism may be less damaging than mass tourism but its potential is limited. It is essentially small scale, and as places become popular there is pressure for larger hotels and better facilities. Once these operations grow it becomes impossible to keep them eco-friendly and sustainable. Costa Rica, once a classic place for ecotourism, now has large luxury hotels and an airport catering for charter flights. The country needs the money generated by tourists and may not have either the expertise or the desire to protect and manage the new developments properly. Can ecotourism really be the answer?

National Parks in England and Wales

National Parks are large areas of beautiful country-side, protected so they can be enjoyed now and in the future. Between 1951 and 1957 ten National Parks were set up in England and Wales. In 1989 the Norfolk Broads was given National Park status, and in 1999 the New Forest was added to the list.

The main aims of National Parks are:
◆ to conserve the natural beauty, wildlife and cultural heritage of the area
◆ to provide a beautiful environment for people to visit in their leisure time
◆ to look after the interests of local people such as farmers and village residents

Over 100 million visits a year are made to National Parks. People can reach these areas easily using main roads and motorways, and summer weekends and Bank Holidays are very busy. The most popular places are often referred to as **honeypot sites**.

National Parks of England and Wales

NORTHUMBERLAND
Newcastle
LAKE DISTRICT
NORTH YORK MOORS
YORKSHIRE DALES
Leeds
Liverpool Manchester
SNOWDONIA
Sheffield
NORFOLK BROADS
PEAK DISTRICT
BRECON BEACONS
Birmingham
Norwich
PEMBROKESHIRE COAST
EXMOOR
Cardiff Bristol London
NEW FOREST HERITAGE AREA
DARTMOOR
Plymouth

N

0   km   200

It is the job of the National Park Authorities to balance the conflicting demands of visitors and local residents. Visitors cause problems such as traffic congestion, footpath erosion and litter, and sometimes even damage people's property. On the other hand, they bring money into the area and jobs are created in shops, pubs and hotels. Farmers may dislike people walking across their land, but can earn money by opening a camp site or farm shop, or providing bed and breakfast. Many people live and work in the National Parks, and industries such as forestry, water storage and quarrying are important, as well as farming and tourism.

The Peak District

The Peak District was the first National Park and was created in 1951. Its central location in the country and proximity to large cities such as Manchester and Sheffield mean that it is also the most visited. About 30 million visits are made to the park each year, mainly by car. Most visitors come for the day but there are around 1 million overnight stays each year.

Visitors in these numbers inevitably cause problems but they also bring business to local people. It is estimated that visitors spend about £137 million in the Peak District each year. The Peak Park Planning Board tries to look after the area by providing car parks, information centres and a local ranger service. It has also resurfaced many footpaths which had been badly damaged by large numbers of tramping feet.

International travel

The map shows some of the most popular holiday destinations for international travellers.

Many countries in Europe are popular. There are three main reasons for this:

♦ A warm sunny climate, sandy beaches or beautiful scenery, as in parts of Spain, France, Italy and Greece.
♦ Interesting things to see and do such as visiting historical buildings or going to theme parks or activity centres. This helps to explain why Britain is a popular destination.
♦ Easy access from other MEDCs. Many Europeans can afford a foreign holiday and choose places they can get to quite easily and cheaply.

The map also shows a number of LEDC countries which are popular holiday destinations,

Main holiday destinations for international tourists

including Mexico, China, Malaysia and Thailand. These countries have built up tourist facilities such as airports, transport and hotels with good food and entertainment so they can attract visitors from MEDCs. Tourism is important because it provides jobs for local people and enables the country to earn valuable foreign currency.

Other LEDCs would also like to use tourism to help them develop but it can cause problems:

♦ Building the infrastructure, such as hotels, roads and an airport, is very expensive.
♦ Mass tourism can damage the environment, for example badly-planned new buildings, pressure on water supplies, waste-disposal problems and damage to the landscape.
♦ Local customs and culture can disappear or be exploited.
♦ Only some parts of the country benefit and other areas remain poor.
♦ Large international tour companies make the greatest profits and these usually go abroad.

Case study: Mass tourism in Ibiza

Before 1960 Ibiza was a beautiful island, with a population of only 30,000. The people were mostly farmers, there were no cars and little communication with the outside world. The island was almost unknown by the people of Spain, let alone the rest of Europe.

In the 1960s and 1970s Ibiza began to build a tourist industry and soon tourism was the island's main industry. People from other parts of Spain moved in to work as builders, waiters or chamber maids, increasing the population. Land along the coast was engulfed by large hotels, bars and clubs. Holiday-makers from Britain, Germany and Scandinavia poured in.

Map showing the location of Ibiza

The island has been popular ever since, but the 1990s have seen a phenomenal rise in the number of visitors. Many are attracted by Ibiza's reputation as a clubbing and dance centre. The population is about 100,000, but on an average day in summer there are over 250,000 people crammed onto an island just 40 km long and 20 km wide. The airport has been enlarged and roads widened, and every year more hotels, apartments, shops, clubs and bars are built. Fishing villages have turned into large resorts, with few restrictions to stop them from spoiling the environment.

There are other problems too:
◆ Large numbers of cars cause traffic congestion and pollution in the peak holiday months.
◆ Over 400 tonnes of rubbish are produced every day in summer. Most ends up in a gigantic dump which has been condemned by the EU because it is contaminating the water table.
◆ There is a serious problem with water supply, and if it were not for two new desalination plants the situation would already be desperate.

Ibiza has probably reached saturation point. There are too few environmental controls. Unless something is done to protect the island in the future, tourists will probably go elsewhere. This type of tourism makes money in the short term, but it is not a sustainable form of development.

🔑 Key words

ecotourism

mass tourism

package holiday

honeypot site

National Park

sustainable development

Test yourself

Complete these captions with as many different points as you can:

There are always lots of visitors here ....

Farmer in Peak District National Park

I have been here for 2 years. I think tourists are ....

Hotel worker in Ibiza

We would like to have more tourists visiting our country but ....

Government official in an LEDC

Examination question

Jobs created by tourism in an LEDC

Jobs	Local people (%)	People from abroad (%)	Total (%)
Hotels: high-paid jobs	1	4	5
Hotels: low-paid jobs	52	1	53
Tour operators: high-paid jobs	2	3	5
Tour operators: low-paid jobs	15	1	16
Other jobs	20	1	21
Total	90	10	100

(a) From the table name two types of jobs mainly done by local people. (1 mark)

(b) Suggest one other job likely to be created by the growth of tourism in the LEDC. (1 mark)

(c) Give two reasons why these jobs are done by local people. (2 marks)

(d) Explain how the multiplier effect works when an industry like tourism grows in an LEDC. (4 marks)

(e) Describe some of the problems created by the development of tourism in LEDCs. (4 marks)

Foundation tier:

(f) (i) Name a tourist area in the EU.

(ii) Explain why this is a popular destination for visitors.

(iii) Describe some of the ways the area has been managed to reduce the damage caused by visitors. (8 marks)

Higher tier:

(f) For a named tourist area in the EU, describe how tourism has been managed to reduce the problems it may cause. (8 marks)

 Exam tip

Try to learn both facts and figures, so when you write about a named area (case study) your answer is precise.

Key word index